STEPPARENTING ESSENTIALS

A Guide to Love, Blend and Survive

MOLLY BARROW PH.D.

Text and Illustrations copyright © 2019 by Molly Barrow
All rights reserved.

StepParenting Essentials: A Guide to Love, Blend and Survive and all related characters and elements are trademarks of Molly Barrow, Ph.D. No part of this publication may be reproduced in whole or in part, or stored in a retrieval system, or transmitted in any form or by any means, electronic, mechanical, photocopying, recording, or otherwise, without written permission of the author, except for the inclusion of brief quotations in a review. For information regarding permission, write to Barringer Publishing, Permissions Department, www.barringerpublishing.com.

Published by Barringer Publishing, Inc. 2019
Editing by James A. Barrow
Layout by Linda Leppert
Illustrations by Eric Pflueger – www.cygnusartsinc.com

ISBN: 978-0-9989069-0-4

Barrow, Molly
StepParenting Essentials: A Guide to Love, Blend and Survive
Printed in the U.S.A.

DEDICATED TO
MAJKK POLARS

INTRODUCTION

StepParenting Essentials provides twenty-five Essential Rules and preventive advice to help the stepparent blend and improve a new family's future. The bioparent must be smart about his or her choice in a partner and be certain that interaction between original and new family members will enhance, not damage, the self-esteem of a stepchild. Co-parenting requires insight and education.

Stepparents Get Their Feelings Hurt in difficult, intermeshed relationships. *StepParenting Essentials* will help you distinguish what to fight for or what to let roll off your back. With these simple solutions, you can reduce common, marital conflicts that psychological studies have shown stress second marriages. Even as an adult, a stepchild may remain hostile without proper blending.

Find Answers to pitfalls that will smooth out family conflict, during the first years of blending children with "new" stepparents. Essential Rules depict difficult stepparenting moments accompanied by psychological explanations and illustrations. You may know the moments—if you do not laugh, then you might cry.

Work on You suggests taking time to work on yourself to help all your relationships improve.

The Matchlines Relationship Test will help you and your spouse quickly identify your relationship's understanding and communication skills. This professional test shows compatibility in many important areas of a relationship. It's like having a year of couples counseling in only a few hours.

10 Essential Couple Conversations navigates the top ten tough subjects every couple needs to discuss to stop future conflict from even getting started!

FOREWORD

StepParenting Essentials is a practical, wise and helpful guide to assist parents and stepparents find a new "normal" amid a blended family. Molly Barrow, Ph.D. uses her twenty-five years of psychotherapy experience to help you protect your new relationship, co-parent with an "ex" after the divorce tempest has passed, and provide the framework to create a respectful, loving home for the children.

Divorce—we do not plan for it. We do not expect it. Yet many of us ended up here. Do not worry. It is simply a new and wonderful beginning. If you are in a new relationship, congratulations, you made it. You worked hard to heal yourself and to provide the stability your children need. Your new partner has seen these positive traits in you and together you will start afresh with some help and wisdom from *StepParenting Essentials.*

Stepparenting is not easy. Mistakes will happen as you bounce back from the trauma of divorce and from the shock of blending. I had a relationship mulligan on the way. It's normal. Each and every touch point with another person is a teaching opportunity for you and your children—and the stepparent of your children.

I have eight kids born between 2002 and 2013 who live with me halftime. I am also a pediatrician and see families go through divorce all too often. Yet, single parents with all numbers and types of kids build new families with new loving partners and are role models for their children. You have, or you will, as well.

Dr. Barrow helped me on my path to a new loving relationship. A relationship that is supportive, honest and nurturing, and healthy for my children. With *StepParenting Essentials* you have the benefit of her knowledge in your backpack, briefcase or bedside to solve problems and pitfalls when blending families.

Pat yourself on the back and be happy you are holding the *StepParenting Essentials* book!

Blessings.

James Brian Thornburg, M.S.M., D.O., P.A., F.A.A.P.
Concierge Pediatric Physician. www.ThornburgPediatrics.com Medical Director, Children's Advocacy Center of Collier County for abused children. Top 7 Innovative Pediatricians in the USA by *Parents Magazine*.

TABLE OF CONTENTS

		Page
25 Essential Rules		11
Rule 1	Nights at the Round Table	13
Rule 2	Road Trip	17
Rule 3	Momma Dearest	21
Rule 4	Gimme Shelter	25
Rule 5	Clean Room	29
Rule 6	Memories	33
Rule 7	Guilt Spoils Rotten	37
Rule 8	The Ex-Files	41
Rule 9	Invisible Sacrifice	45
Rule 10	Some Enchanted Evening	49
Rule 11	Germ Warfare	53
Rule 12	Parental Police	57
Rule 13	Frenemy	61
Rule 14	This Too Shall Pass	65
Rule 15	Sound Barrier	69
Rule 16	Secrets	73

Rule 17	Tu-tu vs. Hotdogs	77
Rule 18	Circling Vultures	81
Rule 19	Three's A Crowd	85
Rule 20	The (Step) Parent Trap	89
Rule 21	Extended Family	93
Rule 22	Let You Eat Cake	97
Rule 23	Take Thumper's Advice	101
Rule 24	Step Pets	105
Rule 25	Blended	109

Work on You   111

The Matchlines Relationship Test   123

10 Essential Couple Conversations 127

Conversation 1	Family Expectations	131
Conversation 2	Communication Strengths	135
Conversation 3	Family Finances	139
Conversation 4	The Ex	143
Conversation 5	Time Allocation	149
Conversation 6	What's Best for Your Stepchild?	155
Conversation 7	Fidelity	163
Conversation 8	Discipline	167
Conversation 9	Religion, Sex & Politics	173
Conversation 10	What Do I Want?	177

StepParenting

Just like you, over twenty million stepparents are struggling to blend "his, hers and ours" into a warm, family unit. Family conflicts and issues don't end at your stepchild's eighteenth birthday. Even adult stepchildren can be difficult. There are more stepfamilies than "original mom and dad" families. Unfortunately, many second marriages fail due to poor communication, infidelity, or stepparenting problems.

Most bad behavior starts with good intentions, yet results in disastrous outcomes. Extreme expectations can rarely be met and create disappointment and shame within the family. Often a bioparent will defend their child to the detriment of their spouse. The family and the marriage can suffer terribly from multiple relationship imbalances.

Knowing when and where to draw the line is critical. Knowing when to let conflict slide is an art.

Nearly all family conflicts can be reduced with the simple solutions you will find in *StepParenting Essentials*. If you believe that stepparenting should just come naturally, realize it does not. Stepparenting is hard work, with many hits and misses. Arm yourself with inside knowledge gathered from the author's thirty years of family counseling experience and save your marriage and children from pain and failure with *StepParenting Essentials.*

25 Essential Rules

"Don't they have good appetites, Honey?"

NIGHTS AT THE ROUND TABLE

RULE 1 ...... Avoid sitting directly across from your stepchild during meals.

PROBLEM .... The sight of messy faces and unwashed hands may ruin your appetite and your meal. Your irritation will show.

STEPPARENT COULD SAY .... "Kids, you can sit next to your mommy, and I will sit way over here across from her."

WHY THIS WILL WORK ... If your stepchild discovers that bad manners annoy you, the manners may get worse. Power and security are constant commodities that all children strive to achieve by monopolizing conversations, interrupting, and demanding to be the center of attention. Your relationship may not withstand the open-mouthed chewing, often enhanced for your benefit, or the rhythmic kicking of your shins.

Young children's table manners are poor, partially due to developmental skills that require coordination.

Assume that your stepchild is doing their best to be good and is trying hard. You may still want to position yourself directly across from your beloved. Your spouse adores their messy little faces—as you may eventually, but for now, you deserve a different view.

An adult conversation is probably impossible without repetitious scolding and correcting. That is no fun. Even if your stepchild does not allow the adults to speak to each other, you can glance occasionally into each other's eyes. Wait for time alone with your spouse rather than lower yourself to compete with toddlers or teens.

Let your stepchild dominate at meals but ask your spouse to set aside quiet adult conversation time just for the two of you.

Make this possible by asking everyone to share nightly chores so this "adult time" has two adults who are awake, focused on each other and listening carefully. Everyone can find "couple time" on the weekends. A few special moments without interruptions should eliminate that feeling of loneliness in the crowd.

"Golden Rule of Blending"
When you and your spouse's households have conflicting rules and behavior, select the higher ground behavior based on your shared values.

Do you both share values of health, cleanliness and frugality? If one of you is more safety conscious, clean, mannerly, honest, thrifty, easy-going, fair, organic or kind—perhaps adopt some of this better behavior—being careful to avoid squashing fun, relaxation or good times.

ROAD TRIP

RULE 2 ...... Take your own car whenever possible.

PROBLEM .... A trip over a few minutes long can push all your buttons and turn you into a screaming demon. Confined spaces increase the impact of an annoying and arguing stepchild.

STEPPARENT COULD SAY .... "You all go on ahead. I don't want to make you late. I'll meet you there."

WHY THIS WILL WORK ... Riding in a car with a hostile teenager, or young stepchild is difficult. If you are cold, they whine they are hot; if you listen to New Age music, they sing television commercial tunes over and over, while your spouse grins at you with incomprehensibly proud pleasure. They wiggle their toes under your seat and use smelly, squeaky invisible ink on their travel books that is probably carcinogenic. If you want to stop for a bathroom, your stepchild complains, and your spouse misses the next exit while telling their child to be quiet. However, if your stepchild must "go," your spouse crosses four lanes and veers off the road in fifteen seconds that leaves you carsick and shaken.

A supportive spouse will smile and know why you want to take your own vehicle and may even wish they could join you.

Spend a few extra dollars on gasoline and take your car when you can. If you must take one car, place your stepchild behind the bioparent.

Prepare well to keep your stepchild occupied and comfortable.

Bring a soft pillow, a favorite stuffed animal, a charged game player, electronic games, a phone charger, some healthy snacks, and water. If you are the passenger, wear headphones and listen to great music or a self-help lecture. Plan as much as you can in advance. Keep even fussy children buckled up as you never know when an accident might happen. Stop at rest areas and let them run. Ensure treats and snacks are healthy and low sugar, and stop every two hours at parks, if you can locate them. When you finally stop at a hotel don't go right to bed. Use your normal bedtime rituals to make children feel secure in a strange place. Read a story, have snack, or play a quiet game.

"Are we there yet?"

Molly Barrow Ph.D.

MOMMA DEAREST

RULE 3 ...... Never compete with the Ex for your stepchild's love.

PROBLEM .... Your stepchild will point out that, "YOU are not my parent, and I love my Dad (or Mom) and don't love you." Loyalty to bioparents lasts forever.

STEPPARENT COULD SAY .... "Kids, you will always love your mom and dad the most. Someday, I hope you will care for me a little, but you never have to stop loving your parents. There is enough love for everyone in our family."

WHY THIS WILL WORK ... You need not take offense at comments designed to show loyalty to the Ex. As your stepchild struggles with whether or not it is OK to like you, they feel guilty and will quickly defend their bioparent's position.

Your stepchild's comments are "pro-parent" and not "anti-stepparent."

Can you hear the love for the bioparent in these comments, or do you only hear the insult to you? "My mom is a better cook than you are," or "My dad is more athletic than you are, and you didn't even make your high school football team," or "I worked with my dad and he taught me how to build a house," or "My mom doesn't have to wear make-up like you do." Sweet . . .

When your spouse observes their child mishandling an interaction with you, they may be able to intervene and change bad behavior. Sometimes, it just takes more time. Because a stepparent is the "new kid," you may approach issues defensively—arms crossed, worried about your authority. See if you can open your heart, your mind, your arms, to allow your stepchild to express their fear, anger and loss. Try to get inside their mind and emotions in a non-threatening, non-defensive, non-territorial approach—just open listening. Don't attempt to replace a bioparent, be an additional parent.

What is especially important is that your feelings are validated by your spouse.

Don't look for validation from the overwhelmed and stressed stepchild. Your spouse may find it tough to believe that their "own sweet child" can be so rude, cold, even mean to a new stepparent. Rather than punish your stepchild, recognize your stepchild's goal is survival, even when they unload their pain on you. They hate their situation, not necessarily you.

> *See, feel, hear their pain and ignore your bruised ego.*

Try to keep your ego out of your relationship with your stepchild. If you just listen without judgment, you may hear the voice of your stepchild struggling to cope with missing a bioparent, rather than what sounds like an attack on you.

Approach the relationship more subtly. Watch for what lights up your stepchild—is it music, a game, math, art, cooking? Start by participating on the fringe of their interest. Bring home a great cooking pan, a new game or a CD. If you jump in too quickly, you may contaminate the interest, so gingerly participate. No strings attached. A little contribution that will demonstrate so much—empowerment, approval, value, friendship, understanding.

Build a healthy adult/child relationship between you and your stepchild separate from your spouse. True bonding may take years.

"This is *my* refrigerator."

GIMME SHELTER

RULE 4 ...... Try to avoid moving into your stepchild's house.

PROBLEM ...... You may need new territory to establish more balanced relationships.

STEPPARENT COULD SAY .... "Let's find a house with more room so that we can call it *our* house."

WHY THIS WILL WORK ... You must establish your space now, or you will forever feel like an outsider. Resist moving into your stepchild's home where you must live with the decorating preferences and "cooties" of the Ex. Although more change may be stressful for your stepchild, additional space (their own room or bathroom) can be a good incentive. Perhaps sell both your homes and buy a new house (in the same school district) that is neutral territory. Even better, if financially possible, build a new house that can help a family bond with a shared project. Include those precious private spaces like an extra bathroom, a study, hobby room, work room or patio that can provide essential escapes. Sometimes just repainting the walls can make a house feel like your home.

> *Territory becomes a critical issue when you have both biochildren and stepchildren.*

A new stepchild in the home displaces biochildren in birth order, power and privilege. Imagine if at work, your supervisor was displaced to mail clerk and the secretary was suddenly your boss. You might feel alarm, anger or discouragement from such a shift in what has been your "normal." Your stepchild, who must share a bedroom with a new step-sibling or follow new rules of a stepparent that don't make sense, may feel the same disorientation.

Your stepchild does not want to share a bathroom with you or their bedroom with a step-sibling either. The issues of privacy and adequate space are important factors not to be overlooked. When lab animals are placed in overcrowded environments, they become anxious and violent.

In rare circumstances, rather than trying to cram two large families into one small house, it may make more sense to remain in separate houses. Harmony and happiness may require a delay in a single-housing plan until finances can accommodate enough space for comfortable living.

Try to keep original family members in shared spaces when possible.

CLEAN ROOM

RULE 5...... Avoid entering your stepchild's bedroom.

PROBLEM....... Even if you are prepared for the shock, never will your status be more clearly and graphically displayed.

STEPPARENT COULD SAY.... "I know you need your privacy; let's make bedrooms private spaces."

WHY THIS WILL WORK... If you enter your stepchild's bedroom, you will see the Ex displayed gloriously throughout the room to include: wedding photos (not yours) of your beloved kissing the Ex, the honeymoon, special mementos of good times before you, relatives you don't know, and if you are lucky, your tiny photo placed behind them all. You think your sense of order is compromised by your stepchild's clutter, and the mess makes you angry, but it is more likely your feelings are hurt. Your stepchild's room is their haven. If the room is bug-free and most of the odor is contained within, then leave their room to the inhabitants. Define minimum hygiene chores required to reduce germs, bugs and odors.

Never remove a bioparent's photos or mementos from your stepchild's room.

Always allow these important memories for your stepchild to be within their private spaces. Save yourself the pain of that stab to your belly and stay out.

The décor should be your stepchild's choice within decency boundaries. Besides, this way perhaps your bedroom and bathroom may be off-limits to your stepchild. That could be a good thing.

Children are naturally manipulative as they initially have no say or power in the direction their lives take. They may be actively trying to sabotage you and sink your marriage. Too frequently, the challenges of parenting innocent stepchildren succeed at ruining second marriages. The statistical failure rate is high, and a problem with children is one of the top three reasons why second marriages fail. However with dedication and knowledge, you can eliminate this threat to your marriage.

Find a connection to your stepchild they can trust.

At first, you may be interacting with your stepchild to make your spouse happy. Your stepchild will sense your false motivation and will react negatively to your fake, nice gestures. In the future, you will truly want to see your stepchild feel happy and your stepchild's reaction to you will change one hundred and eighty degrees. Be real and sincere even if you care only a little bit.

Respect your stepchild's privacy and their past.

MEMORIES

RULE 6...... Never interfere with the natural grief over their broken original family.

PROBLEM....... When your spouse or stepchild grieves for the past, it is typically for the lost family unity, not for the Ex.

STEPPARENT COULD SAY.... "Excuse me, I have to go to the store. I am sorry you are feeling blue. Is there anything I can do?"

WHY THIS WILL WORK... Never deny the original family their private jokes, their sorrow, grief, activities or memories. When your spouse grieves for the past, it is for the dream of family unity, the Norman Rockwell images of family, not for the Ex. Your stepchild has had even greater loss. The grieving process is healthy and makes room for you in their hearts.

The "step" family implies loss, either through a divorce, loss of a relationship, abandonment, or death. A missing bioparent is often idealized and put on a pedestal and their faults forgotten. That is a tough act to follow. You should never be the one to shine reality into the memory. A therapist can intervene to assist with difficult blending and to help keep guilt and misperceptions at bay.

When a traumatic event gets caught in your stepchild's mind and reruns, then these past, painful, memories of what happened years ago cause <u>current</u> pain.

PTSD is a serious mental disorder. If your stepchild's pain showed as bloody wounds on their bodies, would you punish them for crying out? Never!

There will be many moments when you are outside the original family as they share grief, funerals, joy, and memories of favorite restaurants, vacations, photographs of people you do not know, and laughter you will not share. Let them be. You have just as many private memories of your own.

Imagine if you lost what is most dear to you, wouldn't you be angry, hurt and suffer terribly with immeasurable heartbreak? Your stepchild had no say, control, or choice about what they have endured. The bioparents made all the decisions, yet your stepchild pays a terrible price that shifts their statistical numbers drastically toward a more negative future.

A divorce predicts more drug and alcohol use, lower grades, a higher rate of school dropouts, and more interaction with police and school administrators for a child as they struggle to cope with emotional pain.

Does it seem that your stepchild is taking all the turmoil rather well and not demonstrating bad reactions? Perhaps the sweet, quiet stepchild has pushed their enormous feelings down inside, buried due to a lack of coping skills. To hide feelings helps like a surge protector on your computer but is not mentally healthy. The damage will surface eventually. The quiet stepchild is easier to live with, and their trauma may be ignored more than a stepchild who is loudly and abrasively acting out.

<u>All</u> children need help in adjusting to the loss of a bioparent and the addition of a stepparent. Let them grieve.

"I am sorry that I could not get you kids more."

GUILT SPOILS ROTTEN

RULE 7 ...... A budget can help contain the guilt reaction your spouse has for the hurt and damage that their failed relationships or loss of a parent has caused their child.

PROBLEM .... Your spouse may feel agonizing guilt over the loss of their child's bioparent. Guilt can ruin family budgets with indulgent purchases.

STEPPARENT COULD SAY .... "Let's set a budget for holiday, birthday, and vacation spending. Don't worry about gifts for me. Let me help you shop for the kids, we will have fun and stay on our budget."

WHY THIS WILL WORK ... A grieving spouse will have great difficulty with decisions that cause their child more loss and pain. Never expect your spouse to side with you against your stepchild. The parental instinct will usually dominate the new stepparent's opinions. Bioparents are often guilty and conflicted about their divorce and may overcompensate with things. Good parents want to reduce the negative impacts from failed marriages, deceased spouses, or a choice to be a single parent. However, without parental limits in place, they may try to spoil their child in every way possible. Your innocent stepchild soaks up all available attention and funds and then even asks for *more*.

> *Life will unspoil your stepchild with hurts, disappointments, time and maturity.*

For now, let your stepchild be spoiled. Your spouse *needs* to spoil their child to relieve their guilt. Encourage your spouse to have "alone time" with their child often. Your stepchild just wants to be sure that this bioparent won't leave them and still loves them best, worried that you have displaced them.

Ask your spouse to establish a few daily chores for your stepchild to do that will provide a sense of unity and responsibility. Chores may be met with complaints of "child labor" but they are an opportunity to share the workload of the family. Even a small contribution by your stepchild may lessen your resentment for a "self-centered kid." (Self-centeredness is child-appropriate until they become grown-ups). Your stepchild will learn that they are not "royalty" eventually.

Buy yourself something nice for the holidays just in case you are forgotten in the chaos. You deserve it.

THE EX-FILES

RULE 8 ...... Never talk badly about the Ex.

PROBLEM .... You will be blamed and never forgiven, even if it is the truth.

STEPPARENT COULD SAY .... "You are tall like your Dad. I bet you will be good at basketball someday." "Your mommy is part of this family, and we all respect that." "Hey, call your biomom and get her delicious pasta recipe. You and I can cook dinner together tomorrow night."

WHY THIS WILL WORK ... You will be tricked, questioned, and bamboozled into criticizing the Ex. Don't do it. You will be quoted for a decade and blamed with now justifiable attacks. You will be the enemy of the poor, innocent, estranged bioparent. Your stepchild sees the flaws in their parents and loves them despite their disappointments.

Your stepchild will not hate their bioparent, they will hate the one who speaks badly about their bioparent.

Children cannot separate from their bioparent; this is a permanent condition. Your stepchild is half your new beloved spouse and half the aggravating Ex. You must praise "the sum total" of your stepchild, and that means finding nice things to say about the parts of your stepchild that remind you of the Ex as well.

When you criticize the Ex, you put down your stepchild and your spouse for selecting the Ex. Your stepchild deserves to have high self-esteem, to love their bioparents as much as they can, and to feel less conflict in their little belly. Your stepchild cannot like a stepparent who says negative comments about the Ex, the Ex's relatives, or the failure of the Ex to be a good parent.

When the Ex forgets to call a six-year-old on his birthday, never pays child support, or marries a loser, you may want to point out the obvious to your stepchild but shut-up about it. Historical baggage is a land-mine for the stepparent. If you disparage their bioparent, your stepchild feels that comment in their heart.

Never hurt your stepchild with unforgivable words.

"Doesn't he crack you up, what a goof! Ha ha ha!"

INVISIBLE SACRIFICE

RULE 9 ...... Be certain that you give your time, money, and effort as a gift and not as a bribe. Expect nothing back in return.

PROBLEM .... Your spouse cannot read your mind and assumes that you love spending all your time with your stepchild as much as they do.

STEPPARENT COULD SAY .... "I need to work out first, but I will join you for the second half of the game."

WHY THIS WILL WORK ... Successful stepparenting is reflected, not in gratitude, but in the excellent way your grown-up stepchild treats their own children—your future grandchildren. Your gestures of sacrifice and kindness may never be appreciated or even noticed by your stepchild, the Ex, or sometimes even your spouse.

Do not expect your stepchild to reciprocate on your birthday, or with your family. If it is a bribe and they don't do the same for you, then you will feel taken advantage of. If you give a gift of kindness, time or attention, be certain there are no strings attached. A true gift's only reward is to feel great about giving.

When you do something for your stepchild, ask yourself,

"Is this a gift or a bribe?"

Your spouse may not appreciate or notice the effort and control you demonstrate by loving (or sometimes tolerating) your stepchild. Your spouse assumes that you love stepparenting as much as they love parenting. Your spouse wears big rose-colored glasses regarding their child's behavior.

Your stepchild cannot see the big picture—the forest for the trees. Your stepchild only sees how you affect them or stand in the way of what they want. Your stepchild may not notice that you make their bioparent happy and are to be valued rather than treated as an enemy.

Have your spouse explain to their child that you are to be treated with respect like a teacher or a coach. You must demonstrate sincere respect to your stepchild long before you receive a reciprocal level of respect in return.

Even if you develop great stepparenting skills and pour out joyful, loving, fun, kind stepparenting, your stepchild may not be emotionally ready to receive.

Divorce-damage can take years to heal.

Sometimes your self-esteem hits the skids. You feel ignored, disrespected, and invisible. So many decisions are dictated by your spouse, your stepchild's needs, or an Ex you don't know. The powerlessness is painful, and anger seethes beneath your smile. Maybe you feel like giving up.

Wait. Try to focus on the good you are putting out, not the trickle of benefits returning to you. As time passes, your sensitivity to every slight will nearly disappear, your stepchild will improve a little, and it will work. Be grateful right now to be part of a *family*, even if you feel like just a "friend" or an "observer" at first.

SOME ENCHANTED EVENING

RULE 10... Make time for romance with your spouse, not just sex.

PROBLEM....... The stress of blending with your stepchild can dominate all private adult conversations. Romantic love requires time, effort, and prioritization to keep the thrill and fantasy alive. A great marriage requires energy, focus, and at least sometimes, prioritization, or it may grow cold.

STEPPARENT COULD SAY.... "Darling, we need a break! Let's pretend we do not have any troubles, or kids, and make our date just about us. Tonight, we are single, sexy and in love. Your mom's coming over to sit with the kids."

WHY THIS WILL WORK... You may not have the romantic luxury of alone time like a couple without the responsibilities of children; however, every love deserves some romantic moments and happy conversation. Children can drain emotional reservoirs leaving parents bone-dry with nothing left for each other. Parenting can be the antithesis of romance, if you let it. A smart couple will make time for romance.

Carve out alone time for a quiet dinner for two and rekindle your romance.

If you can arrange a babysitter you trust and if your spouse isn't too tired from running errands for the kids, maybe, just maybe, you can arrange a tender night out together.

Try to avoid discussing your stepchild when on a date with your spouse.

Within moments of pulling away from your home, your spouse may want to discuss a few important family issues. Agree beforehand to ignore troubling topics tonight. Without realizing what is happening, a couple can slip slowly into the cliché of child-dominated, romance and affection-lacking, exhausted parents. You may want to avoid alcohol as one often becomes more argumentative when inebriated, and the last thing you need is an argument on a stolen, rare, romantic night.

When you are finally alone on a date, focus on how wonderful your partner is and leave all your problems and issues for another time.

Empty nesters may long for interaction with their grown children who are busy with their own lives. The older couple may not have the passion, energy, hormone levels, or sexual interest they once had for each other. Their relationship needs a "new baby" to share that can be in the form of a puppy, project, or new business. Some couples may adopt a child. This benefits the child and revitalizes the family.

Relationships that survive are because two people worked hard, compromised, listened well, kept learning, and sacrificed for love.

GERM WARFARE

RULE 11 ... Avoid sharing a bathroom with your stepchild.

PROBLEM .... You need personal boundaries and some privacy.

STEPPARENT COULD SAY .... "The kids should have their own bathroom."

WHY THIS WILL WORK ... Sure signs of repulsion are putting toilet paper on the seat like in a gas station bathroom. Then you begin to use antibacterial sprays. Soon you hide your personal items, toothbrush, hairbrush, and contact solution. Communes failed because unrelated people cannot share bathrooms. The stepchild feels the same way about you.

If you are building a home or have space to remodel, multiple bathrooms are more important than a formal living room or dining room that few families will use. A stepchild can gain possession of items by simply touching them and contaminating them. A bioparent has fewer issues with changing a dirty diaper, bouts with the flu, or sharing personal items and won't have the same "ick reaction."

> *Establish your private spaces early on, before your stepchild lays claim to the entire house.*

Sometimes when finances are tight, shared personal spaces get even tighter. On vacation, in an attempt to save money, you may choose a single hotel room crowding the family tightly together. Normal bodily functions, burping, gas, tooth brushing, sounds, and smells from the bathroom are inescapable and a little maddening. Consider a small vacation home that may be equal in price to a hotel, and far superior in space as a solution.

At home and when traveling, a quick wipe down of surfaces with a disinfectant cloth reduces flu germs, impetigo, strep and staph and makes good hygiene sense. It also relieves the squeamishness from sharing spaces with the "unwashed."

Do you dread the moment your stepchild enters the front door? Are you happier and more relaxed when your stepchild leaves the home? Do you isolate yourself in your room to avoid any contact you might have? Are you having trouble standing the very presence of your stepchild?

These feelings are from a lack of acceptance on your part that your spouse came as a "package deal." Let go of any fantasy of a life with just you and your beloved and your kids but without their child, pets, Ex or baggage. Who do you think you are to be so unfair in your relationship? Your stepchild feels, sees, and senses your disdain, and so does your partner. Your partner cannot and will not separate from their child. You are setting yourself up for the collapse of your marriage.

Embrace the "package."
It will grow on you.

Molly Barrow Ph.D.

PARENTAL POLICE

RULE 12... Do not discipline your stepchild for the first few years.

PROBLEM....... The stepparent who wants to control and discipline their stepchild has little real influence at first and may be too harsh.

STEPPARENT COULD SAY.... "You are the boss of your biokids and I'll be the boss of my biokids. I will support your decisions, and I hope that you will support my decisions." Tell the misbehaving stepchild, "Wait until your Mom (or Dad) gets home!"

WHY THIS WILL WORK... This stall has worked for generations. Loving your spouse means you are supportive, understanding, and helpful. It does not mean you take over the whole parenting job. When you try too hard, your stepchild will resent your interference, and your spouse may feel inadequate like you think you know more. You do not know more about your stepchild then the bioparents do, and you never will. Trust the inside knowledge your spouse has about their child and defer to your spouse's decisions.

You have zero power or influence in the first years, so let the bioparent handle discipline.

If you attempt to discipline your stepchild, you will be too tough on them just because they annoy you. Quietly and lovingly ask your spouse to control their offspring and to give consequences for their child's bad behavior. Although your spouse will discipline only halfway, it is still more effective than your best shot.

Weak parents who cannot teach rules or boundaries, often create an ill-mannered, insecure child. Offer to take a parenting class together to improve the family dynamics. The best definition of discipline is to teach, not punish or shame. You cannot take back words spoken in anger. Belittling, defensive, mean-spirited words cut and maim. Just stop. Don't say unforgivable words.

Take time to think, escape, compose yourself and return to the higher self you aspire to be.

Avoid discipline standoffs. Eventually, you will have real power (in a few years), and your stepchild will care.

Can you listen? Really listen? Even the youngest stepchild will resent you if you don't give them an opportunity to be *fully heard*. When your stepchild's explanations seem outlandish, remember most conflict and defensiveness disappear when both sides feel they were adequately heard. Sometimes, a family meeting can be an opportunity to express problems and find solutions before they escalate into battles.

Rather than disagree with your spouse in front of your stepchild, wait to decide until you can converse in private about important issues and then present your decisions as quiet, calm, and united adults.

FRENEMY

RULE 13... Try hard to be friends with the Ex.

PROBLEM....... The Ex is probably threatened by you and not really your friend as they fight for funds and parenting time, change plans and take your spouse to court—again.

STEPPARENT COULD SAY.... "We had planned a road trip to Yellowstone with the kids, but if you want them all summer, we could change our plans." (Think to yourself—vacation alone with your spouse).

WHY THIS WILL WORK... The Ex probably will never appreciate your help in raising their child, sacrificing the best years of your life, your hard-earned money, or any of the ways you try to help. The Ex is threatened by everything you do and truly believes that you want to steal the "little darlings" away.

The Ex will never be an ex-parent.

Respect the Ex's wishes about what they think is age-appropriate, the best health decisions or about discipline, etc. You are in the business of childrearing and are a subordinate to the bioparents on most child topics. This position may pinch ... but it is true for all stepparents and comes with the job.

The Ex may complicate every situation, change agreements, and be righteously intolerant and inflexible if you should ask for something from them that is outside the court agreement. However, once the divorce is final, parents must throw out their emotional baggage and transition to "lifelong partners" connected in the business of raising a healthy, happy, emotionally stable child.

If you can be civil, or even friendly, then the next twenty years of shared school events, health decisions and celebrations at graduations, weddings, and births will be drama-free and more fun for everyone.

That means all parties should show no jealousy, no flaunting a new partner, no fighting, no sarcasm or belittling, no using the child as your messenger or go-between. Set firm boundaries to avoid falling back into old relationships. Be friendly, but business-like, not lover-like, in interactions with the Exs.

Give the Ex lots of quality time with your stepchild while you spend quality time getting to know your spouse more intimately.

THIS TOO SHALL PASS

RULE 14... Avoid sexual discussions, interactions, jokes or excessive flattery with your stepchild.

PROBLEM....... Sex is an agonizingly embarrassing, awkward, enticing and sometimes frightening subject for kids.

STEPPARENT COULD SAY.... "I think it is supposed to rain tonight but should clear up for tomorrow's soccer game."

WHY THIS WILL WORK... Never have demonstrative PDAs or scary passionate encounters with their bioparent in front of your stepchild … keep it affectionate. Some families can talk or joke openly about sex and feel comfortable. Most Americans cannot. A young stepchild may be frightened, confused or made overly curious when exposed to sexuality. If they learn something interesting, they will most likely share their new-found knowledge at school and wind up punished.

A sexually developing child may try out their flirtations on everyone—the parent, the handyman, the maid or you.

Bioparents find their innocent child who mimics adult behavior to be normal, funny or just annoying and often ignores the behavior. Stepparents may flip out about sexual behavior, and their reaction creates a tense, awkward mess. Or, worse, the stepparent participates.

Developing their sexual wings is the right of all fledgling children. This is natural, and a necessary passage to adulthood. Some children are precocious and demonstrate adult behavior at a surprisingly young age. Some kids only care about sports or hobbies into their twenties.

Try to remember how strange and powerful the subject of sex was when you were young and innocent.

Your stepson may shadow-box with you in a playful challenge. Your stepdaughter may copy the way her mother treats you. Whatever a kid does is usually a passing phase. Ignore this as much as possible and tell them to go and bother their bioparent.

Let your stepchild initiate any intimacy and define their physical boundaries with you.

As a general rule, do not touch, hug, or kiss a stepchild first. You are in the "stranger" category for a long time. Even babies and toddlers let you know when they don't want to be held or touched by someone whom they don't trust yet. If you reach for a baby and the baby's hand goes to its mouth, that is a screaming, "No!" in baby talk. When you try to hug a toddler, and they shove you away, you have crossed their line. Never force a child to hug or kiss a "smelly," old relative either.

The fantastic metamorphosis from child to adult is a sporadic, awkward, embarrassing process when a child's body, that has been dependable for over a decade, changes. Growth spurts, menstruation, body odor, facial blemishes, new hair growth, breasts, and hips are not usually welcomed by kids. Teens need all the support and encouragement they can get to keep their self-esteem from crashing. They need to hear that they are on the right track for a healthy brain and body and a wonderful future ... to give them hope.

Mr. Fred Rogers said it best— "I like you just the way you are."

SOUND BARRIER

RULE 15... Protect yourself from your stepchild's noise whenever possible.

PROBLEM....... Your stepchild's noise is like "fingernails on a chalkboard." Your spouse does not hear the noise, only you do.

STEPPARENT COULD SAY.... "I added some extra soundproofing in the walls, so they would have a quiet space to do their homework."

WHY THIS WILL WORK... Never have adjoining walls with your stepchild. The din will drive you out of your mind. You will hide, closing doors between you to escape the high-C, shrill, non-stop chattering, of nonsense subjects strung together in a non-ending run-on sentence that rises and falls like waves, beginning with, "And," and slowing at, "So." When the discourse finally ebbs, your spouse asks their child another question, and you are forced to seek peace and quiet elsewhere.

Molly Barrow Ph.D.

A happy child chatters, spins in circles, runs, climbs, talks loudly, sings loudly, laughs loudly, and bangs rhythmically on tabletops and dances.

You want a happy stepchild. However, so much noise can make you go bonkers. Don't ignore this problem. Take the time and money to insulate your home from noise with carpet, wallboard, weather-proofing strips, and foam, noise-reducing padding on all adjoining walls with your stepchild. Carry earbuds or earplugs as protection. Play your music and calm down. Stop yelling at them to be quiet. Let the children be children but protect your nerves.

Toxic input includes people who leave you drained, TV shows full of conflict, yelling and fake tension, and computer killing-games that all add to the dysfunction in a home and can be reduced.

Set a regular time of the day for *quiet*. Turn off all the negative input entering your sacred home space.

The "Quiet Family Time" (QTF) needs to be pre-planned and announced days in advance. QFT is an opportunity to pull out some "good ole' days" activities like charades, card games, skill games, water balloon battles, playing musical instruments together, shooting some hoops, or simply a walk around the block. Keep it light and enjoyable, not a punishment or highly competitive. Your stepchild's brain will process all the previous electronic input, and their anxiety level will drop—as will yours. Shared laughter and fun are a great way to heal from stress damage.

All electronics should be turned off an hour before your stepchild's (and your) bedtime to help them fall asleep.

"*Pleez* don't tell Dad I pierced my *tongue*."

SECRETS

RULE 16... Never let your stepchild win your allegiance away from your spouse.

PROBLEM....... Your stepchild wants to tell you something important in private. Avoid becoming the sole confidant of your stepchild.

STEPPARENT COULD SAY.... "I am sorry, but I will not keep a secret from your parents."

WHY THIS WILL WORK... Although you may be pleased that your stepchild trusts you and wants to confide in you, you will regret sharing a secret with your stepchild. They will tell you horrific things and then make you promise not to tell your spouse. Listening quietly to your stepchild validates them, which is good, but let your stepchild know you cannot withhold important information from your spouse.

Important information means drugs, alcohol, sex, crimes, health, bullying, and debt—all must be shared with your spouse.

Your spouse will resent you for withholding important information about your stepchild. Your job is to build a solid, trusting relationship with your spouse first as the family foundation. Good relationships with your stepchild only develop when trust and shared respect exist between the adults. Your stepchild will feel stabilized, safe and more secure if they are unsuccessful at putting a wedge between you and your spouse. If you fall for secrets, it will separate you from your spouse, and eventually, backfire.

Everything will become your fault.

Your stepchild will still try to entangle you given an opportunity because they want power over adults. Let your spouse decide how to handle the situation, and you back up your spouse's decision. If your spouse is off base, too harsh or too nonchalant, let them know your opinion in private in a quiet, non-threatening conversation. Your spouse may not change their position, but you have a right to politely express your opinion when it is <u>important</u>.

Although you may be flattered at first by the apparent selection of you by your stepchild due to your brilliant intelligence, wit and experience, it is because you are probably viewed as the weakest link. Avoid entering into a dangerous triangle. If the "secret" is OK, then why isn't your stepchild sharing this information with you and their bioparent? Embedded in your stepchild's selection of you as their confidant is a future disaster for you.

If the "secret" that your stepchild shares with you is that they hate you, then you can calmly respond, "Wow, that really hurts my feelings because I like you. I hope someday you will like me, too."

If you expect these comments from your stepchild and prepare for them, then it won't hurt so much, and you won't react like a crazy person.

Give them time to genuinely care for you.

TU-TU VS. HOT DOGS

RULE 17... Never schedule dates with your spouse during your stepchild's events.

PROBLEM....... The child's numerous school and extracurricular activities are not optional for their bioparent.

STEPPARENT COULD SAY.... "No problem, Hon. I need some time with my friends; I'll call Rick. He can have your Yankees-Red Sox game ticket. I will attend the next recital."

WHY THIS WILL WORK... You are not "Number One." You are, and always will be, the second team. This may make you feel like number two, but your stepchild's needs take precedence—almost always, because it is assumed that your needs can wait.

Do not make a mistake by testing this. You won't like the result if you force the issue, and make your spouse choose. However, "Number Two" is far better than alone.

Molly Barrow Ph.D.

Check the "Family Schedule" first before planning any adult activities or surprises.

If your spouse has worked all day, run errands, struggled with a crabby child, and arrived home to a messy house with dinner next on the agenda, they are frazzled. Your suggestion of "Hey, let's go to the gym and workout!" will be irritating and insensitive. Instead, have empathy for the demands of your spouse's schedule and energy level.

Tread carefully as your spouse is already stretched thin, conflicted and doubting that all that they do is still not good enough for you or the family. Give your spouse a break and put no added pressure on them to be a *super-spouse*.

Your spouse is in the unenviable position of coordinating child activities with the Ex. Sports practices, rehearsals, math bowl, classroom activities and performances may fall on the Ex's time and must be organized or they won't happen.

Prepare a family schedule for visitation schedules, school holidays, events, parties, etc. and keep each other informed of any changes to the schedule. Online schedules will update all parties simultaneously.

Plan ahead!

CIRCLING VULTURES

RULE 18... Never allow the competition to work the kid angle.

PROBLEM....... Predatory singles will use your stepchild to entice your spouse.

STEPPARENT COULD SAY.... "We are so proud of our family, we couldn't be happier."

WHY THIS WILL WORK... Attend parent-teacher nights and other school events even if you are bored to tears. It is a jungle out there, and your spouse is fair prey for predatory parents looking for a stepparent for their children. They will pretend to adore your angelic stepchild and imply that they would make a better stepparent than crabby, complaining, unreasonable you. Your vulnerable spouse may fall for it. You must defend your territory until you get this stepparenting thing right. Unscrupulous people use children to approach parents all the time.

Advertisers target their ads to children to get to the parent. A parent's feelings of insecurity about their child may be an opening for a competitor, one who is more interested in seducing rather than parenting.

Recognize when someone's name keeps coming up frequently regarding your stepchild. Promises of happiness, athletic or scholarly opportunities, or extra attention for the child may be a strategy to attract the parent.

Watch for a "face-off" when a rival's body and shoulders face your spouse's directly, and they block you out with their body language. It is a subtle exclusion but can be telling if it happens frequently and with only one person. Politely mention your observation to your spouse and explain that you sense an ulterior motive may be in play. Assume your spouse is unaware and innocent but ask your beloved to protect your relationship a little better in the future.

Never allow predatory singles to fawn over your stepchild.

If you get a bad feeling about a person who is showing interest in your stepchild, say something. A child is vulnerable to an adult's or older teen's influence. Your stepchild will adopt beliefs and behavior from whomever they are exposed to and establish habits and brand preferences that can last a lifetime.

If Grandpa is chain-smoking around your stepchild, if Mom has her 5pm whiskey every day or Dad always drinks Pepsi, never

Coke, there is an excellent chance your stepchild will adopt some or all of these habits.

Children spend twice as much time in front of a television than they do in a classroom according to the Advertising Education Foundation. Children influence nearly fifty percent of the purchases made by a family. Influence is all around your spouse and stepchild from other sources.

Give your opinion and share your knowledge when it feels right.

Cut out the middle man!

THREE'S A CROWD

RULE 19... Never get involved in original family arguments.

PROBLEM ...... You do not know what the origin, backstory, blame or fair resolution is to their feuds. Stay out of the middle.

STEPPARENT COULD SAY.... "You need to work this out between the two of you. I wouldn't dream of interfering."

WHY THIS WILL WORK... Do you actually know what they are fighting about? Usually, family conflict is some power or love issue from long ago. Never intervene in original family arguments unless there is bloodshed.

If you get in a triangular argument between two people, you could be hated by both. It is such a lose-lose position.

A triangular argument is the pulling in of a third party to referee, or worse, to side with one party. This makes a compromise more difficult, and each side will feel betrayed by you.

Interference by the stepparent limits the ability of your spouse and your stepchild to resolve their issues. Wait to be asked for your views and opinions of disagreements. Your stepchild may resent your butting in, and your spouse may feel like you have usurped their position.

Let them work out their conflicts on their own.

Forcing a child to be in the dangerous position of "messenger" is abusive to the child as they may say something that angers the adult, yet the child has no understanding or defenses.

Your stepchild should not become the messenger for your spouse or the Ex who are avoiding speaking to each other.

A well-functioning family rarely has arguments. No family is perfect, and many conflicts blow up into arguments. Arguments become shouting, tearful, anguished, emotional breakdowns when calm, listening, fair communication has failed. Strive to reduce or eliminate all arguments.

Molly Barrow Ph.D.

© Disney

THE (STEP) PARENT TRAP

RULE 20... Beware of some children's movies.

PROBLEM....... Walt must have had an issue with stepparents. The family laughs hysterically as the villainous stepparent is eradicated, and the bioparents are reunited. Your feelings may get hurt.

STEPPARENT COULD SAY.... "I'm going to walk the dog, I need some exercise."

WHY THIS WILL WORK... Click your heels and go somewhere else. Your stepchild's desire for parental reunification will last forever. The plot of classic children's films is often about victimizing the stepparent, so the original parents can get back together. These movies are fun for everyone, except the stepparent.

This same theme of "how to get rid of you and get the bioparents back together" is running through your stepchild's mind.

This theme is natural for children who feel they have lost a parent through a divorce, and you cannot change that. However, you don't have to listen to joyful laughter as a "slimed" stepparent gets annihilated in a movie.

Experts have found that the majority of films that feature a stepparent character portray that character negatively. Society associates negative behavior like abuse or molestation with a stepparent more often than with a bioparent.

Negative perceptions of stepparenting may be the result of exposure to these films as well as similar characters found in the literature children read.

The role of the "wicked stepmother" in films and literature abound. The predominant myth is one of fear, cruelty, and jealousy that endures. The victims in these stories are often rescued by heroic males. Your stepchild has been exposed to these universal myths hundreds of times, in their books and movies. This type of toxic myth may permeate your relationship with your stepchild.

The power of this lingering myth causes many women to have a more difficult time with acceptance by children than does a stepfather. A stepmother must fight this stereotype head-on when she joins a new family.

Stereotypes of stepparents depicted in children's films do a disservice to the stepchild who may be wrestling with the relationship with their stepparent. Explain gently to your stepchild you are not a character in a movie and that you have *good* and bad qualities.

EXTENDED FAMILY

RULE 21... Include grandparents as often as possible.

PROBLEM....... Your stepchild needs all the love and stability they can find.

STEPPARENT COULD SAY.... "People who love you are welcome in our home."

WHY THIS WILL WORK... Grandparents can provide love, nurturing, easy discipline, teach manners, and give joy to your stepchild. Offer invitations to *all* extended family to attend events, birthday parties, illnesses, or ceremonies that involve your stepchild. Yes, that includes even the Ex and some weird relatives. Do you remember your heartbreak if your parent or grandparent missed your little programs or games? These group events might be difficult on everyone—except your stepchild.

Your stepchild will heal when divorced bioparents are civil and friendly.

True, your attendance probably goes unnoticed except by your spouse (but that matters the most, right?).

Engage all willing grandparents to help stabilize your stepchild. Intense positive interaction makes a stepchild easier to live with and often more mannerly and calmer. Extended family is essential for your stepchild who may cling desperately to their bioparent after a divorce. A nurturing grandparent can release your spouse to have more energy and time for you and your biochildren.

Someday your stepchild may even thank you for this one. So, fake it, roll with it, see the humor in the situation … whatever it takes. The beloved relatives are your stepchild's, not yours or your spouse's domain. These special family love moments are not about you; they are for your stepchild.

Joyfully share your stepchild's life with loving extended family as an investment in their mental health.

If the grandparent demonstrates favoritism and defies your family rule of fairness, gently mention to them how much favoritism hurts. Blood relationships typically have stronger ties. Grandparents may be motivated to take a grand-stepchild along with their bio-grandchildren on trips or overnights. However, grandparents in their '60s, '70s or '80s may have limited energy for the stress of young children even though their desire to do more is there.

Rather than insist on equality with grandparent relationships, help your stepchild find other sources of positive attention like clubs, team sports, and charity work. Many elderly and lonely people would enjoy being "adopted" by the stepchild whose own grandparents are absent.

Molly Barrow, Ph.D.

Let me eat MY cake.

LET YOU EAT CAKE

RULE 22... Never give up your basic human rights to gain points.

PROBLEM....... Sometimes you must stand your ground to gain your stepchild's respect and establish balance in your relationships.

STEPPARENT COULD SAY.... "I want to be a role model of fair and caring stepparenting and sometimes that means I must be assertive about my rights, as well as yours. Therefore, this last piece of cake is MINE!"

WHY THIS WILL WORK... Stepchildren don't appreciate a stepparent's sacrifices until they are about thirty and you are old. Occasionally demonstrate a moderate defense of your rights and space as a human being.

If you always give in hoping to gain points with your stepchild, they will view you as a pushover and lose respect for you.

Meanwhile, hold your position if something matters to you.

If you have taken on the family role of "good-time stepparent," when you do finally put your foot down, you may not be noticed. If you have allowed your stepchild to speak or treat you rudely, it may be difficult to earn back respect. There is a balance that is tricky. Although you cannot jump into an existing family system and "fix" all their dysfunction, on the other hand, you cannot let your rights as a member of the family disappear either.

Maintain a non-aggressive presence who does not allow abuse from anyone in the family.

Often, older stepchildren see their inheritance at risk when a new spouse enters the picture. A prenuptial agreement protects you, your stepchild and the parent from confusion and hurt feelings regarding inheritances. Their parent should be clear and open about how the wealth and property will be divided among family members to avoid secret suspicion, sabotage, and resentment. Great wealth is unnecessary to trigger greed and jealousy. Sibling relationships can be permanently destroyed, by squabbling over "the vase mother promised to ME!"

Adult stepchildren's negative attitude and behavior may be difficult to comprehend. They may feel rejected by their parent, jealous of their newfound happiness or embarrassed by the sexual life of an older parent. Every new person added to the family shifts the status quo. Your spouse may have zero control over an adult stepchild's animosity toward you, but your spouse must try. Knowing your spouse has your back when those subtle slights hit your heart minimizes the damage.

These "baby-adults" are still struggling with childhood issues and questioning whether they are loved and appreciated.

TAKE THUMPER'S ADVICE

RULE 23... Never make your stepchild the brunt of your jokes, shame or put them down.

PROBLEM....... Your sense of humor may verge on mean and hurt your tender, sensitive stepchild. Childhood shame lasts *forever*, never to be forgotten or forgiven, and disparages their self-worth.

STEPPARENT COULD SAY.... "Let's all be kind to each other in thoughts, words, and deeds."

WHY THIS WILL WORK... Do you share laughter with another person by finding surprise and delight in an unexpected situation, or does your sense of humor require a victim to make a joke funny?

If you can't say something nice, be silent.

Your spouse will not find a victimizing joke about your stepchild funny. If you are asked why you told that mean joke or laughed at your stepchild, choose to save your marriage, apologize, and try to be kind. Learn to honor your stepchild's right to have self-esteem and dignity. You cannot joke around with your stepchild the same way as you do with your biokids, or in the same manner that your spouse can. Leave the jokes to comedians.

There is always an intention and motivation behind an action or words.

What was your intention here? Beware the pulley system—the philosophy of bullies. When a bully puts you down, then in some twisted logic, they think their "cool" goes up. It does not work that way. Instead, each time the bully speaks, acts or implies a put-down that victimizes someone, the bully goes down in value. Funny jokes can be offensive and often require a victim. When jokes ridicule "powerless" people, they are cruel, not funny.

Before you say a critical word or have a critical thought, remember you are bringing a ton of baggage into all your relationships, too.

Show the compassion you expect others to show you. Words matter. Call a boy a thief and he will steal. Call your stepchild a miracle and watch them flourish.

Sometimes a stepparent will try to bond with their stepchild by disparaging and ganging up on the bioparent. Making fun of the bioparent is often "the boys" against mom or the "girls" against dad. The stepchild will follow the lead of the stepparent and enjoy the freedom to be disrespectful and act superior to an authority figure. This immature behavior by the stepparent is self-destructive and wrong in so many ways. Victimizing your spouse is confusing and hurtful for the marital relationship and erodes parental control of the child. There are far better ways to interact with your stepchild than to isolate and ridicule a bioparent.

Lead with your kind words, not your mean jokes.

STEP PETS

RULE 24... Learn to love your stepchild's pet, too

PROBLEM....... In many families, the pet is a family member. To reject the pet will cause terribly hurt feelings.

STEPPARENT COULD SAY.... "Nice doggy, good kitty."

WHY THIS WILL WORK... When joining an existing family, the family pet is part of the whole package. Imagine choosing only one stepchild to ostracize and reject or to find one stepchild so distasteful that you want to get rid of its smell, dirt, sounds, or dander. This is how your stepchild will see it if you openly dislike the family pet.

When blending two family pets like your dog and your spouses' cat, integrate the two animals slowly, using smells, your calm, reassuring voices, and quiet playtime. The first meeting is crucial, and any negativity may be long-lasting. If sleeping arrangements change, give the pet extra love, treats, and attention, to make up for the loss of your bed.

A pet can help bring a family together with shared laughter and enjoyment of the pet's antics.

Allergies are a problem for many people. Alternatives may be antihistamines, or perhaps, Grandma will adopt the family pet, but only if it is a medical necessity.

Your stepchild's affection for their pet must be of primary consideration and would be a source of profound loss if separated.

More loss is the last thing your stepchild needs.

Blending pets within the family can trigger emotions and become a political issue between theirs and ours. Rather than focusing on the challenges of being a pet owner, try to remember how many benefits there are to a child who has been hurt. A pet can be a source of comfort for a lonely, anxious or depressed child.

The benefits of owning a pet are numerous from lowering your blood pressure, reducing stress, stimulating oxytocin, and providing unconditional love.

Caring for and walking the pet could be a shared activity with your stepchild, offering both protection for your stepchild, acceptance of the step pet and an opportunity to be together. Sometimes through loving, laughing, and playing with your step pet, your stepchild will learn to accept and like you, too.

The step pet could be a short-cut to a harmonious family.

BLENDED

RULE 25... Believe every day you *will* blend.

PROBLEM....... Blending a family may take years, especially with an older stepchild.

STEPPARENT COULD SAY.... "Just another bump in the road, but we will be a great family someday soon."

WHY THIS WILL WORK... Stepparenting requires courage, stamina, and great love for your spouse. A comfortable blending may take several years, but you will do the seemingly impossible. One day you will realize you have grown to love each other and have somehow built a family despite all the problems and stress.

The realization won't come with a lot of fanfare. Perhaps it is the moment when your stepchild calls you "Mom" or "Dad" on their own. Maybe one day your stepchild chooses to ride with you in your car instead of their bioparent's car. Maybe you are invited to play catch or receive a Mother's Day or Father's Day card that says love or thank you. You just feel differently. The awkwardness is gone. The resentment is forgotten. The expectations have been exceeded.

Now you see a person whom you love and the word stepchild changes to "my son" or "my daughter."

You may even reminisce and laugh with your spouse at what you had to go through. Every memory shared gives you a common history that binds you emotionally, even the disastrous vacations, the midnight trip to bail your stepchild out of jail, and many ruined family holidays. You have learned to adapt and roll with the punches.

You realize that you don't want to be anywhere else in the world than with <u>your</u> family.

Work on You

Take a moment to think about who You are. Whose voice is speaking to you in your memory? Who is giving you the words that you speak? See if any of the following apply to you.

How Were You Parented?

First, take an honest look at your own readiness to join in these convoluted stepparenting relationships. Were you abused, abandoned, molested, raised by alcoholics or addicts? Have you worked hard to overcome your childhood trauma before you pass on inherited bad behavior to your stepchild or biochild? Or have you suppressed the reality of your childhood and never speak of it? Childhood trauma may still be there pulling your behavior strings and making you a puppet of your past. Have you gone to therapy and told the whole truth? You began life as a perfect child before others hurt you or bad luck tripped you. You deserve love, freedom from trauma and acceptance. We all do.

How Do You Parent Yourself?

Do you give in to that the cookie, coffee, drink, cigarette, wrong partner, repeatedly and then whine about it? One way to determine if you experienced suppressed unforgiven and unresolved childhood trauma is to examine your own possible addictions to alcohol, drugs, sex, porn, work, obsessive cleaning, organizing and controlling behavior. If you are clinging to these "blankies," you may be holding back "remembering," and holding in old, rotting trauma. Let it go. Get help, if you need to, and start today to live clean, new and free.

Can You Be Different?

How different can you afford to be and still be accepted by your family? All species on the planet are attracted to similarities. Differences often repel and cause fear and anxiety. A tribe depends on their ability to recognize friend from foe. Over eons, there has been tight conformity to the "same," that created illusions of safety and relief from the suspicious anxiety of "different." That is why we seek friends and partners who reflect ourselves, look like our relatives, and espouse the same philosophies.

Your Right to be Extraordinary

You and your stepchild have a total right and opportunity to be eccentric and different within the small space of time we call our lives. You live because your ancestors cared and parented sufficiently. You have just as much right to exist, vote, laugh and feel love as does any great self-appointed royalty. You are more than just an individual; you have history! Your DNA goes back to the first people on earth. You have a connection with all the people who have ever lived and strived from the beginning of human history, a link in a wonderful chain.

Each time you protect your freedom to be you, you also help protect all people who desire freedom. If someone tries to deny you the freedom to design your life as you see fit, then you must fight loudly with your voice, your vote, your money, and your work to protect the right to live your special life assertively—in both your intimate relationships and in your larger societal relationships. Your secret weapon is to be flexible and allow others to be different. If you allow your stepchild and spouse to be uniquely different, even eccentric, you gain the freedom to be your unique self, too. Embrace differences in others, do not fear them.

Learn to negotiate these rights and be proud to differ from the status quo. Whatever is different about you, you must voice your opinion and have a "say." Because each time you do, the prison door opens a little more for oppressed people everywhere.

How Do You Define Yourself?

Write a description of who you are and who you want to become. Did you list attributes or accomplishments? Did you list good family heritage, male, tall, handsome, and blond? Realize that you had nothing to do with any such attributes. Or did you write kind, hard-working, an athlete, loyal, spiritual, patient, fair? These descriptions take hard work and commitment on your part. When you achieve accomplishments like these, they are your claim to high self-esteem. Teach your stepchild to value their accomplishments, both small and large, and to enjoy the long, hard journey required to master skills.

What Are Your Personal Goals and Values?

What do you value about your life? Are your values ambiguous? Hazy? What do you want?

When you are rock solid in this area of your life, pervasive change happens. Can you list your goals and values in a hierarchy of what is the most important? If you are deeply religious, you may list your relationship with God first. Perhaps you put family first. Did you include your health near the top? Without your health, you will not have much time to work on your other values and goals. Number these values from (1) to (16), with (1) being the most important. Compare your hierarchy with your spouse.

__ Your Health
__ Your Family's Health
__ Children as a Priority
__ Peace of Mind
__ Safety
__ Clean World, Food, and Water
__ Honesty and Integrity
__ Politically Active
__ Physically Fit
__ Devout
__ Loved
__ In Love
__ Financially Secure
__ Sacrificing now for a better future
__ Freedom from Tyranny
__ Well-read/Educated

Think of each of these values in the big picture, from a global perspective right down to your own neighborhood and living room. How do you apply your values to your everyday actions?

Are You in A Group?

Are you a member of an association? List the groups with which you align yourself. Sometimes this will reveal hidden prejudices that rarely surface, yet subtly influence your behavior. Try to stay slightly separated from your groups, parties, and associations. Remain first an individual who may differ from all the regulations of membership and conformity required just to "belong."

Blame Game

If you blame someone else, like the world, your partner, your bad parents or a punishing God because you are not happy, then you will remain glued to your excuses and the blame game. To get control of your own life means you stop blaming others and begin to make changes for the better.

If you want your life to be different, then you must be the one to make changes—in you.

Can I?

Do you feel powerless? You are powerful. The power to change is already in you. Other people are busy with their own lives. They will walk right over you and not even notice you are waiting for someone to make you happy, to fix your pain or to balance your checkbook. Take your hits bravely, make the best of a situation or leave it, then be happy as you work toward your goals.

What is the point of a defeatist attitude mostly concerned with looking innocent? "I didn't do it." Would you want those words to be a synopsis of an entire irresponsible life? After today, be eager to say, "I did it!" regarding your life decisions. Repeat often, "I gladly take responsibility for changing my life." Take responsibility for you, stand up, move forward and clean up any mess you make yourself.

Attitude

A totally positive attitude is a lie. So is a negative attitude. Neither is the absolute truth. However, positive attracts positive; therefore, that is the game to play. A negative attitude is self-defeating, immature, and frankly, not smart, because it creates a negative pull, spreading the negative attitude to people around you. When you ask these people for help, they are turned off by your "stink-face." Both attitudes are contagious. So, which one do you want to spread around you?

How you bounce back from adversity is what matters.

Are you are projecting resentment and frustration to everyone you meet because life is not going as you planned? It is time to grow up and get on your "smiley-face." Life never goes as planned (deep down you already knew that).

Practice Positivity

You need to jump and dodge the obstacles of life until you get it right. If you naively expect a smooth run out of life, then frustration and disappointment will overwhelm you and keep you locked into childish behavior. Stay open to personally growing until your behavior and thoughts are healthy. Your relationships will be better because of the work you do on *You* now. Learn to take baby steps while preparing for the backlash of resistance from family and friends that surfaces whenever their loved one begins to change. You may have to struggle to present your positive attitude at first. It is the smart choice because even if you hate your life, you will pull positive energy towards you from others. Eventually, you will feel positive for real.

Commitment

Can you commit to yourself, to your goals, your causes, and to the people you love?

Commitment to yourself means you work hard for your dreams and goals. Commitment starts in the morning and runs until you fall asleep. Your accomplishments reflect your commitment because even with some bad luck along the way, committed people can become president, an expert, famous and/or happy. You can rarely attain big goals without commitment as a top value.

Choose Your Style

You alone must decide if you must wear high heels or a tie to be good enough to do your work. You decide if it is right to be poor in money and rich in time. You decide if you leave work to attend your step kid's ball game, even if it costs a half-a-day's pay. You decide if it is right to invite your Ex and your spouse to the same holiday party. Try it. It might work, and if it does, your stepchild will love having both of their parents around at the same time.

Try to avoid deliberately stepping on anyone else's toes or attempting to convert them to your own form of weirdness.

Be Free

Let other people be who they are—unless by your good example they want to be more like you, and then if asked, help them to understand your values and perspectives. Allow yourself to be unique; or better yet, celebrate your inherent uniqueness in all the ways that make you happy.

To have freedom of speech, to have a unique religion or non-religion, to have a traditional or non-traditional family, to work for a big company or your own small business, to be involved in your community or to live on a mountaintop, and to have the sacred right to be a little weird, are all hard-earned constitutional rights. Many people gave their lives to protect your freedom and rights.

Vigilantly protect your right to be all you can be, in your family, your community, and for everyone else. Before the "real you" gets too lost in what everyone else tells you who you "have to be," become a rebel with a cause. Or you might never find who you are again.

Are You Assertive?

The stronger, more aggressive party will trudge right over a passive person to get what they want. If you are passive, then it is your fault for lying down on the floor and letting them "walk" on your rights. If you lie there like a doormat, <u>everyone</u> will walk all over you. The weaker partner must become stronger, to the point of balance and equity, or the relationship will become horribly unbalanced, and the whole relationship system will fail. Will the strong-willed partner notice the inequity of the relationship and help the weaker one? No, usually not.

Not Enough Things?

Do you feel ashamed or frustrated because you do not currently have a new car, and a great job, and a new house, and many friends? Is everyone supposed to have it all, great job, great family, great looks, and a great life? Residual role expectations can leave you exhausted. Step out of the chase. Leave the rat race and enjoy living. Study minimalism and get back to basics and simplicity.

Too Many Roles?

Social pressures once defined a woman in her relationship and defined men in their employment. Many men and women found their "designated role" to be unfulfilling. Society's glossy promises of happiness within rigidly designated roles rarely holds true.

Men and women naturally want the closeness of a family and good relationships. They also want to succeed in their vocation and be free to pursue their dreams. Usually, a conflict in designated roles ensues: Mother vs. Entrepreneur? Father vs. Husband? Good Daughter vs. Girlfriend? Devout Member of the Faithful vs. Party Animal? Executive vs. Athlete? How many hats do you wear? Limit the roles you take on and accept only the most important ones to you. Find the hat that fits you best and wear it proudly.

No More Lies.

How about integrity? Without integrity in both public and private actions, the direction you take will have little to do with a positive outcome. A liar gets caught eventually. Tell the truth.

Now, perhaps you know yourself a little better. How will you apply the skills you have learned? Can you raise your self-esteem by selecting different values? When you incorporate good values that are your preferences, you will be proud of yourself, and so will your family. Right now, begin to stand for something great. Be someone whom you admire.

"Life moves pretty fast. If you don't stop and look around once in a while, you could miss it."

Ferris Bueller's Day Off
(Paramount)

What words would your stepchild use to describe you?

- Controlling
- Over-disciplining, punishing
- Aloof
- Crossing boundaries
- Forcing intimacy that is not there yet
- Jealously competitive
- Demeaning
- Sarcastic
- Rude
- Hot-tempered
- Immature
- Unfair
- Loud yelling
- Liar
- Manipulating
- Cheap
- Withholds love and affection
- Resentful
- Demands respect
- Too religious
- Bully
- Embarrassing—crude jokes, over-sexed
- Selfish
- Immoral

- Fun
- Fair
- Listens
- Understanding
- Patient
- Responsible
- Secure
- Trustworthy
- Good person
- Kind to animals
- Appropriate behavior
- Gentle
- Healthy
- Good communicator
- Easygoing
- Hard worker
- Good for their parent
- Agreeable
- Smart
- Supportive
- Dependable
- Generous
- Confident

The MATCHLINES Relationship Test

Why take the Matchlines Relationship Test?

The Matchlines Relationship Test© is a confidential online analysis designed by Dr. Molly Barrow for you and your spouse to take. The test consists of true/false questions and takes forty-five minutes to complete. The Matchlines program will compare your answers with your spouse's answers. Five graphs are *instantly* created that represent your relationship. This bird's-eye view of your strengths and potential conflict areas is an evaluation similar to couples counseling, only your results are fast, accurate and inexpensive. A willingness to know how to fix problems with your communication and interaction could save your marriage.

If you discover where a problem is hiding *before* it becomes destructive, you can prevent future problems—like having a preventative medical test. The answers are <u>confidential</u>. No one including your spouse will see your answers, so tell the truth. When you exit the Matchlines program, your answers are erased. The cost of the test is $25.00.

Print the graphs with a *color printer* and also print the seventeen-page bonus material. The graphs will clarify where and why conflict may occur in all your relationships, old and new.

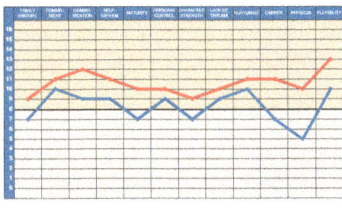

MatchlinesTest.com

10 Essential Couple Conversations

We Need to Talk

This section contains ten essential conflict-reducing conversations that every couple should have before and during the blending process. These are the hard conversations; the ones new lovers try to avoid because they are afraid to rock the boat.

Rather than bury your head in the sand, start these conversations, knowing that your feelings, experience, and opinions will change as your relationship matures. Today you may be dealing with toddler tantrums. Years later, you may still deal with a rude thirty-year-old stepchild. Learning how to be a good communicator is essential for marital happiness and strong functional families.

These Ten Essential Conversations will help you and your spouse handle marital and stepparenting challenges as a team.

Essential Couple Conversation 1

Family Expectations

What vision of the future for your new family do you foresee? Are you laughing together, having a card game, tearing up at graduations, awards, and weddings? Or, do you sit apart from the others, tight-bellied and resentful, hoping for time alone with your spouse? You may have a fantasy of what child-rearing is like if you have no child of your own. You may be missing the instinctual protective halo that bioparents have for their child, or lack the experience and sensitivity to your stepchild's unique personality. Ask yourself if you want your stepchild to be happy, obedient, or invisible?

Bad Roommates

A little closer to the reality of the first years of stepparenting is to prepare yourself to potentially be taken advantage of by passive-aggressive, bad roommates who try to undermine you. You are entering into a difficult job that is every day, all day, unpaid labor, often unappreciated, with little reciprocity. The exciting part is that you have a new chance at love and the family life you have desired. This will require all you possess in patience, strength of character, and love. If you can survive the rough spots, the end result is worth it!

You do not need to be the best at anything. You are good enough as you are. You bring many good qualities and some bad to the new family. You have some strengths and prejudices, opinions and experience. You will use all of you to raise your stepchild, to develop your path, while learning from your mistakes. Allow yourself your feelings and design your unique role. A stepparent gets points simply for hanging in there.

Roles

Do you have antiquated visions of your spouse's role in the marriage? Should she clean, cook, care for family and then become a sexual delight. Should he pay all the bills, throw the football and make all the decisions for everyone? To keep this new family boat from sinking everyone needs to be prepared to do all jobs, take care of each other and give more than humanly possible.

Children irrationally hope they can change the past, make reality go away, and recapture a Norman Rockwellian version of what was.

Often desperate and lacking few coping skills, your stepchild may turn their angst against you and fight you for dominance in every interaction. Your spouse may be deaf and blind to these assaults, but you feel them as a kick in the gut. Will you become hostile and defensive, or do you have the capacity for compassion for your stepchild and spouse, both of whom may have been terribly hurt and still suffer daily?

Believe

Does your spouse believe you when you say your stepchild tests your patience and is out to get you?

Or does your spouse think that you are exaggerating and that you should adore your stepchild in the same way a bioparent naturally does? Will your spouse support you when you feel you are drowning in the thankless job of stepparenting and forgive you when fed up, frustrated, annoyed, selfish and crabby? It happens, and even with the best intentions, it is difficult to be a good stepparent all of the time.

A blended family is an uneven relationship. A stepparent is second team, not first team. If you cannot be comfortable with taking a backseat to the original family, then the marriage will be filled with conflict. Your role is not to break open an existing "system," but to *blend*.

Love is not enough to make a new family system work. It takes determination, patience, study and often counseling to make it through rough waters.

Hope-fully

If you have expectations for yourself or your family, that are unfair, too high, too many, or not meaningful to others, then you may live with disappointment. Disappointment multiplies and spreads, poisoning a positive attitude. If you switch out disappointment to feel gratitude (even if your situation is not in good shape), your world will shift to a higher plain, out of the daily muck. Lift your eyes toward hope and aspiration for your family's future. A finer place to live, certainly.

Essential Couple Conversation 2

Communication Strengths

The ability to communicate calmly, honestly and respectfully, makes a family system work. Tolerance is essential because you are jammed into a single space, like a pressure cooker. Minor conflicts, offenses, little betrayals, misunderstandings, and jealousy present themselves often and cause sometimes ridiculous arguments. If your stepchild is growing up badly, that is for their bioparents and grandparents to deal with. However, if a bike scratches your Porsche, yup, that is for you to ask to be made whole.

Words of Love

Unconditional parental love is a force of nature that stepparents don't automatically acquire because they have fallen in love with a bioparent—any more than you automatically love your new mother-in-law. But disliking your mother-in-law is far more acceptable than acknowledging that you don't yet feel close to your stepchild. It is a two-way street. The unconditional love that your stepchild feels for their bioparent isn't coming your way for many years, but it can eventually. Your stepchild will construct part of the meaning of "love" by what they see and experience in your care.

When you need to vent, begin with reassurance, "I love you,

and I am committed to our family, but I am feeling frustrated with ..." This approach will stop your spouse from becoming defensive and rendered unable to listen or hear you. Say a truthful "I" statement without sarcasm or exaggeration. "I think this ..." Never say, "You are ..." or, "They always ..." Start your sentence with, "I want" or "I need to" rather than, "They must."

The best fix for most of your relationship problems is to take a communication class or series of counseling sessions to improve your communication skills.

Check your Body Language

The tone of your voice, body language and timing can communicate demeaning, shaming and blaming messages to a hyper-sensitive stepchild and defensive spouse. Sometimes a note on the refrigerator is safer than talking to an explosive teenage stepchild. The silent family member who emanates anger but never communicates fears confrontation. Like a bad apple, just one sullen seething person can bring down the happy mood of the whole family. Learn to communicate while problems are small rather than exploding suddenly. Separate family issues that are major from the minor ones that are just annoying, or none of your business.

Beginners Luck

When your spouse tries to give you well-intentioned advice on how to be a better stepparent, try not to hear it as criticism. Instead, admit you are a novice. Listen and study and read to improve your skills. Your spouse can assist by reminding your stepchild to be forgiving toward you, as you learn how to improve your stepparenting techniques. Sometimes you will be wrong and should not have yelled, punished, not listened or stormed out of the house. It is OK to explain that you are learning to be a great stepparent. Say you are sorry and will try harder to be better. Never be the bad apple of your family.

Accept different points of view as a great first step toward good communication. Often differences are minimized or ignored when a relationship is new and in a rapturous cloud of adoration. These differences resurface later and loom like storm clouds weighing down a couple's euphoria.

Take time to learn how to communicate fairly and gently to strengthen your relationship. If you argue or debate with a partner, you may win the battle but lose the war as your partner may feel disregarded and bullied.

Invest in your relationship by learning how to listen, hear and accept each other's true self.

Senses

Sometimes if you listen carefully, you can identify sense-words that can help another person hear you better. Does your stepchild say **sight** expressions like, "I see," "Look," or "My vision is ..." or do they use **hearing** words like, "I hear you," "Sounds like ..." or "Listen to this ..."? Some people say **touch/feel** words, "I feel like ... ," "I sense that ...," "I am touched by what ..."

If you identify and switch to using your stepchild's or spouse's "sense words" to communicate your message, they will comprehend you much better.

Essential Couple Conversation 3

Family Finances

Develop your family's financial budget before or early in your marriage. Show each other all your financial details, good and bad. Evaluate the loss of existing lifetime alimony to your spouse if your relationship fails, or how bills will be paid if someone dies.

Factor in the future impacts to your finances from illness, loss of a business, a major lawsuit, or a new baby.

Budget

Work out your budget together. If you pool your money and share expenses, use a percentage of your income, such as each contributes 25% to household expenses, 10% to savings and 2% to vacations. If your spouse makes twice the money you do, it is not fair for you to pay half the expenses and have little left for your discretionary spending. Expensive items for your stepchild like new computers, camps, cars or college can make a stepparent feel resentful if these items are not listed in the family budget. Does the family budget pay an allowance for chores or are those expected?

Seismic Shifts

How would a shift in visitation impact your finances? Do you want children in your life every day or can you coordinate a child's visitations, so you have every other week child-free? How would sole custody affect your time and finances? If visitation agreements change and your stepchild becomes full-time in your household, will that put a strain on your ability to work from home? Is your spouse staying on the budget? Have you or your spouse tried to buy the love of your stepchild or tried to heal trauma with frivolous gifts, indulgences or things? Things will not heal a grieving child.

More Children

Kids are wonderful, complicated, and expensive. Would one or both of you like to adopt a child? Does your spouse want to have another baby? Do you?

Alimony and Child Support

Your spouse may be paying a fortune to the Ex in alimony or child support. These decisions were made long before you entered the picture, so those expenses are not your money or concern. You may need to make more of your own money, if you want to have more purchasing power or security. You could get a part-time job and hire a sweet, patient nanny rather than force yourself into the role of a stay-at-home, unhappy stepparent who must pinch pennies.

Time Costs Money

If you have older teenagers who need less parental supervision, parents can work longer hours, start a new business or go back to school. However, young children need a parent at home as much as possible. Not a depressed person staring at their phone, but a parent who is engaged, one who remembers how to play and laugh. Sometimes having more money buys the freedom to stay home with your stepchild, sometimes all it takes is to purchase fewer things—for now. The "minimalism" concept versus "competing with all your rich friends" can release you to enjoy the pleasure of *time* with your family.

The wealth jointly owned in a relationship must be divided equitably, or else resentment will begin to divide the relationship.

Equality

Some people think of money as an extension of themselves. Some use money to control others. Are you living in a one-sided dictatorship—with a king or queen who is sovereign and owns all, surrounded by their dependent loyal subjects—or is the family dollar divided equitably and representative of your needs and other family members?

If you give up control of money decisions to your partner, then they are the boss, and you are the secretary. When you offer one partner a position of entitlement and power, it inevitably goes to their head. Soon the inequity of the rules in your relationship will spread pervasively throughout the house and make your partner feel they may do whatever "the boss" wants to. You gave up your power and started this inequity-downslide. Protect and keep your relationship balanced with as much equity as possible given your unique circumstances.

Financial equity is a key component of a healthy relationship.

Essential Couple Conversation 4

The Ex

Insecurity with the Ex and your stepchild's lack of affection for you can fuel resentment and fear in the new stepparent. Your stepchild did not get a divorce. There is no divorce of your stepchild and bioparent. Let the bioparents love their kids their way if it is not hurtful. Your stepchild may eventually seem to give up on a bad bioparent but carry longing in their heart for the redemption of dad or mom. Even if you are a perfect stepparent, or even if your stepchild never knew their bioparent, the fantasy of the child-parent loving relationship lingers.

Loss

After a divorce, your stepchild often loses their bioparent half the month, or sometimes completely. Children want their bioparents to reunite miraculously, and stepparents are in the way of that strong wish. Your stepchild feels powerless to change what has happened to them, often blames themselves and most want their bioparents back together in an attempt to heal their aching heart.

Grief is debilitating, and suicide and depression are real concerns for

your stepchild who has experienced divorce and loss.

It does not matter if the Ex is dysfunctional, disturbed, mentally ill, distant or even deceased, your stepchild loves their mother and father, and they will for the rest of their lives. Even if your stepchild has never met their bioparent, they will create a fantasy about how wonderful that bioparent must be.

A conflicted relationship between bioparents who are trying to co-parent demonstrates ignorance of the extreme damage that battling parents do to a child.

Green

You may feel jealous of the bond that bioparents share. The Ex may make decisions that cause you to alter your plans, weekends or vacations. You and your stepchild are powerless to change the situation. It may feel awkward at first, but it is so much better for the whole family, especially your stepchild if bioparents can communicate in a friendly way. Assist in peaceful, positive interactions, by never demonstrating an "attitude" or jealousy if your spouse can manage civil, or even pleasant, communication with the Ex.

The bioparents must maintain good communication to enable compromise in conflicted situations.

Conflicted bioparent-interaction keeps your spouse yoked for life to a mortal enemy, and that is awful for everyone. Allow the Ex to participate in all of your stepchild's events. If the Ex acts horribly and ruins your stepchild's birthday, that will certainly annoy your stepchild. That annoyance and disappointment may be preferable to the emptiness and lonely despair of not having a bioparent attend. Besides bad behavior reflects on the Ex, not you.

Taking the high road of inclusion is still the right choice.

Emptiness

The child will see their parent's failings and feel bad, but the vacancy that a bad Ex leaves can never be filled completely even by a great stepparent. The hurt and loss remain. You don't ever need to point out their father or mother's inexcusable behavior. Illogically, your stepchild will forgive the erring parent many times and may not forgive you a thing. This is not a popularity contest. It is simply the truth and so difficult for your stepchild to understand. Your stepchild will blame themselves by believing that they are somehow lacking and not good enough to be loved when their bioparent acts badly or worse does not show up.

The Ex is not your business, but they are a minefield of hurt for your stepchild. Even when your stepchild says negative comments about their parent, you must never join in or contribute to parental criticism. Listen to their complaints but don't join in. Any bad thing you say will be remembered, repeated and never forgiven.

After your spouse has weathered the agony of divorce, custody, psychological assessments, court, emotional breakdowns, and financial disagreements, the bioparents must continue to co-parent as partners through childhood and grandchildren.

The Ex will call and text your spouse, stop by, and join family events, be at the hospital if your stepchild is hurt or sick, attend doctor's visits and all-important school events. Wouldn't it be better if you all can act like adults and move forward as "friendly" co-parents for your stepchild's sake? This is what a good, responsible partner in parenting should do. Civility is a good goal for all.

Your stepchild should never hear a bad word about their bioparent from you or anyone else. Your stepchild will take that criticism deep in their heart, and those negative words will become part of what defines the stepchild, not the erring bioparent. If you criticize the Ex, it only hurts your stepchild.

Don't do it, ever. You cannot control the Ex's parenting time. If the Ex is a bad parent, your stepchild already knows it. Never tread into a bioparent's territory or attempt to tell them how to parent unless abuse, molestation or neglect exist. Your spouse must intervene and fight the Ex if your stepchild's health or welfare is in danger.

You married your spouse and his or her "package" of relatives. You cannot get rid of the Ex, the grandparents, family, old friends, cousins, and extended family—all who may openly dislike innocent you. Your stepchild may have been down this road before with one or more stepfamilies and divorces. Expect them to be courteous to you and little more. Attempting to force a feeling on another person never works. Time and good stepparenting will earn you the love and respect you want. Your best efforts to love and parent your stepchild may be fiercely rejected because of loyalty to the Ex. For instance, if you insist on being called Dad or Mom, you are stepping into bioparent territory, and your stepchild will not like you for it. Even if a bioparent is missing, terrible, or deceased, your stepchild will defend their parent.

> *Inclusion and communicating with the Ex is the best strategy to reduce future family conflict (and to stay out of court).*

Someday, in their late twenties, your stepchild may realize how much you gave and sacrificed for them and you could even get a thank you.

Molly Barrow Ph.D.

Essential Couple Conversation 5

Time Allocation

Does your spouse expect you to attend all of your stepchild's events or are you allowed to choose your level of participation? A healthy couple has interests and experiences that don't always include both partners. A co-dependent relationship is stifling and becomes boring. Doing new things without your spouse, refreshes you and the relationship. Take time away from the family to remember who you are and what you enjoy. When you bring your happy energy back to the family, your new, exciting experiences add value to all.

Communicate your participation limits.

Are you anxious and depressed while you attend another stepchild event? Are you holding on to resentment, ready to burst and try to boss everyone around with your novel ideas that likely will not work? Everyone will resent your interference. Ready to blow your top? Pick a handful of things that are important to you, a weekly date night, a fixed bedtime, more privacy, reduced noise level. Is your birthday sacred regardless of any school event? State what matters to you and ask your spouse to help you achieve what matters the most to you.

Balance

Your spouse is not a mind reader and already time-compromised. Time allotted to your relationship is beneficial to you and your spouse and necessary to build a strong foundation for the family. Unfortunately, your stepchild will feel each minute they do not dominate as a loss rather than a gain. Finding the balance of good stepparenting often requires a sacrifice of the marital bliss and freedom that newlyweds enjoy. Share time with each other at Little League games and socialize with other couples with children as much as you can.

How long are you willing to give your new family to blend successfully—a few months, a year, or five years? Or as long as it takes?

Daily Schedule

Work on a daily schedule together. Agree on regular bedtimes and mealtimes. Kids need to eat dinner earlier, closer to 5:00 even with a snack right after school and will become cranky if they wait to eat until 7:00. Why force your stepchild to go against their biology to conform to your schedule? Separate mealtimes are ok. Maybe make quality family-time after meals instead of the old-fashioned sit-down dinners.

Calm or Cortisol

Are you always late or always punctual and let time control your mood? If you are stuck in traffic, how could you use the moments? You can honk or make rude gestures, turn red in the face, and then die from excess cortisol very soon. Or, you can select a new song while you idle, do some isometric exercises while you sit in the car, share a commiserate shoulder shrug and a smile with the pierced kid in the jacked-up truck next to you. It is your call. When you are in line at the bank are you frustrated and impatient? Discontent is like a bad smell emanating from your facial expressions. Alternatively, are you standing in line well, using the best posture you know? Are you ready to make the teller's day wonderful? These mundane experiences happening right now are your life. Stop waiting for "I'll be happy when X happens."

Work Styles

We each have different patterns of work. Some people have momentary flashes of brilliance, and then they go blank for a while—consider them thoroughbred racehorses. Some people have steady, consistent medium levels of output—consider them Morgan workhorses. Some people appear to be stubbornly standing still while they invent new ideas, call them Einstein-like mules. Some people create in their dreams or while sailing on a sailboat. Some people work frantically for hours at an office and accomplish nothing. If you are trying to be a nine-to-five person and you are built for flash speed, then you are squeezing into work shoes that do not fit.

Are you an attention-deficit person with a messy desk, all surfaces piled high and drawers left open? Are you an obsessive-compulsive neat-freak, or do you land somewhere in between? Recognize your style of work and be content to accomplish what you can in your own comfort zone, without all the stress of faking a persona you are not. Your spouse has their style of working, as does your stepchild with their homework and chores. Try to become immune to criticism from other people with different work styles. Avoid criticizing others for their innate brain-functioning and their inability to change.

One advantage of self-employment is that you can be more of who you are by working within your own rhythms. Our patterns of work reflect the plethora of intelligence we have. Some people are smart with time units. Some people are smart with logic. Some could never maneuver in New York City, yet know the weather from smelling the breeze. Everyone is talented and smart in their unique ways.

Piece of Pie

Make a pie chart with sixteen slices to represent your waking hours. Mark out hours spent eating, showering, commuting, at your job, parenting time, special needs of friends or geriatric relatives, and maintaining things like your car, house, boat, pet, rental homes, yard, and laundry.

You can see graphically how little time there is left for romance, social relaxation, hobbies, writing a novel, or learning to dance and just how precious those remaining moments are.

Time allotment should represent your goals and values.

If you have several children in your household, try to spend time with individual children separately from the group to build a stronger personal relationship with each other. Make a big effort to keep these small and frequent moments evenly distributed throughout the family. Try to be fair and avoid favoritism with the "easier" children. Maybe help one child with homework, take one child to the store with you or walk the dog with another.

These small allotments of your time mean a great deal to a child and can turn into family traditions such as, "We always watch the World Series together" or "We always pick out the Christmas tree together."

Essential Couple Conversation 6

What's Best for Your Stepchild?

Acceptance

Give non-judgmental freedom to your stepchild to be a loud, silly, active little individual. What yearning lies in their heart? Challenge your stepchild slightly beyond their developmental ability. Too much demand and your stepchild will internalize failure and lose self-esteem. Not enough challenge gives a false bravado. If you choose your stepchild's activities as part of your goals, the family unit gets stronger, and you learn to have fun in new ways.

Listen

Your stepchild's opinions, dreams, and goals deserve to be listened to and taken seriously. Ninety-nine percent of today's urgent needs and desires will not still be there a month from now. Your stepchild is mercurial and will flow from idea to idea. If you stifle this brain flow and ridicule, disagree, or shame their ideas, they cannot grow up with self-esteem or reach their full potential. Your stepchild has a calling and deserves to fulfill that dream or desire without adults telling them their dream is impossible to achieve, because of the adult's insecurities, personal limitations, fears or conflicts. Let them fly their way within a lawful and moral framework.

Attachment

Secure childhood attachments lead to independence and positive, committed relationships as adults. Never take away your stepchild's security objects like "the blanket" or stuffed animal. Never. If your stepchild is hanging on to an object, then they need it emotionally. The more trauma your stepchild has experienced, the more delayed their maturation. Some kids will need that stuffed animal in middle school. Help them feel more secure with positive interaction, not depriving them of a potentially crucial piece of their security. Your stepchild gains security from attachments. If attachments are broken, your stepchild may become an adult who lacks empathy, cannot maintain a long-lasting relationship and lives angry at the world. Not fun to live with. This is why parents have driven hours to retrieve the forgotten blanket or stuffed animal on family vacations. One day that toy or object won't matter anymore as in the theme of the movie, *Toy Story*. Attachments will move to favorite friends, or even perhaps to you.

Stability

Stability is essential to your stepchild's mental health. Transitions and change, even good change, cause stress in your stepchild. Avoid moving to a new school district unless there is no other option. Your stepchild would lose their friends, their history, their status and their habits. Seeking new friends often drops your stepchild to a lower level of social groups. Your stepchild works hard to belong to a group, and the loss of their group can be devastating. How stable are you for your stepchild? If your spouse suddenly died, are you committed to going the distance, to continue to parent your stepchild and to contribute financially, or would you pass them off to another relative?

Sincerity

Your stepchild can recognize when you are faking it. Fake love never works. If you treat your stepchild kindly and fairly, then mutual respect will develop over time, and maybe even love. Your stepchild is not going to meet your needs for love, trust, and friendship, but you can help meet their needs for these important emotions. Even if you are a terrific parent to your kids, you may not be a good stepparent, just yet. However, a sincere approach to your stepchild will be noticed and appreciated.

Trust

Try to avoid surprises. Establishment of the "Family Rules" are essential. Post on the refrigerator a list of behaviors you expect from all children in the household and the consequences for breaking the rules. Make most of them easy to accomplish but have two or three that are essential to parental sanity and important to your stepchild's safety or development. A BIG lie, stealing, leaving the house at night, smoking, drugs or drinking are important and need to be on the list for middle school and high school children. Kids under eight-years-old struggle with imagination vs. reality and sometimes don't realize they are telling a lie—so go easy on them until they develop an understanding of truth.

Kids must know the rules and punishment <u>before</u>, not after the infraction.

Clear rules, expectations and fair consequences provide a solid floor beneath your stepchild's feet. When the bioparents went through the chaos of divorce, your stepchild may have been neglected and developed some bad habits. Given a trusting and fair household, your stepchild will thrive emotionally, and their behavior will improve. Most bad habits will be replaced with good ones, especially in a younger stepchild.

Kid Timing

School-age children need nine to ten hours of sleep nightly. Feed them when they are hungry. They can pay attention for about thirty minutes before they need to move around. Schools should adapt to children's mental and physical needs and not vice versa. Playtime is as essential to development as book time.

Bad, stupid parents foolishly punish hungry, crabby, exhausted children.

When you give your stepchild a sugary soda or ice cream, then you must expect them to act manic and bounce all over the house. You poisoned their brains with a ton of sugar, or yellow or red food coloring, or that blue slush, so punish yourself, not them, when subsequently, the next few hours go very badly.

Time-Outs

Bad behavior earns a time-out equal to the age of your stepchild. A time-out is sitting in a chair with no television, sounds or distractions. For a three-year-old, three minutes is forever. The timing begins when they are sitting quietly in the chair and understand why they are being punished. After the time is up, ask them to tell you why they received a time-out. After a time-out is completed, then they may play again. Your stepchild can adjust their behavior at your household, schools, grandma's or on the soccer field with no damage.

Long or harsh punishments teach only hatred and resentment and will backfire badly.

No child was ever a better person because they were left alone in a dark room to cry themselves to sleep. The goal is to socialize a potentially wild, violent, ill-mannered little person, and help them become a good adult. This process may take eighteen years or more. Brace yourself.

Teach by Example

If you lie, your stepchild will lie. If you smoke or drink, odds are so will they. If you cheat or change rules in your favor, expect the same from the rest of the family. Lead by your good choices instead of crooked, cheater choices. Distract and whisper to them rather than yell. Say it once. Don't go over the infraction again, and again.

Kids are not the Same

A parent rarely loves, understands or enjoys all of their children the same. Stepfamilies are even more diverse. You may never love your stepchild as you love your own. Your stepchild is acutely aware of this inequity. Interactions, feelings and even the sound of your laughter is more intimate with your child than with your stepchild. Bonding is innate, and nature demands it, or all young would die from neglect. If you pretend you are equal, your stepchild knows you are not and will feel betrayed. Be more open about the time it takes to love someone. Explain that your relationship is growing and right now unfair, but you hope someday not to feel any differently about your stepchild than you do your biochild.

At least that is honest, and your stepchild will feel hopeful, rather than deceived. Let your spouse have the final say on the rules and consequences as a stepparent will typically tend to over-punish, lacking a sensitivity chip to the nuances of your stepchild's unique suffering. This is especially true if your stepchild has ADHD or is on the autism spectrum. What may look like "on purpose" to you, probably is not. This child will often truthfully say, "I forgot." Punishing a special needs child for their handicap is like punishing a blind child for bumping into a wall.

If you are stepparenting a special needs child, become thoroughly educated about your stepchild's challenges and understand their struggles.

Rule Breaking

The "Family Rules" will be broken. Your stepchild needs to make their own mistakes and handle tough situations to grow up to become a responsible adult. Know that when you write up the Rules, that most will be broken or tested. The point of discipline is not to gain the stepparent's comfort level, but rather to help socialize a human being with teaching, not severe punishments and strict obedience. Use "Pack Mentality" to your advantage by saying, "<u>Our family</u> doesn't hurt animals," (or lie, steal, hit, etc.).

Belonging, as an incentive to good behavior, works.

Regression

Most people like to be babied occasionally, like when they are sick, or hurting from loss or disappointment, when they were not invited to a party, broke up with their boyfriend or did not make the team. The same goes for adults.

A guilt-ridden spouse may appear to be overly attentive to their child. Your spouse and stepchild may have been through trauma you can never fathom, and they are bound together tightly, leaving little room for the stepparent to join in.

Over-attentiveness can create over-dependence in your stepchild.

Generally, if your stepchild can tie their own shoelaces, the parent should not tie the shoelaces for them. Exceptions are always allowed. Accept that you don't know what's best for your stepchild. You can watch outside all the drama even if is directed at you, staying removed and observe what your stepchild is struggling with today. The issues will shift to something different next month. So, avoid making a big deal out of today's crisis issue or jumping in "to fix" your stepchild.

Your stepchild under stress will regress. A potty-trained child may have accidents; a stutter may develop, nail-biting, and cutting are all signs of severe stress. Don't punish. Find and eliminate the stress.

If a child is being molested, bullied or abused, they may tell only <u>one</u> person. If that person does not protect them, they will resign themselves to the abuse continuing. Believe your stepchild and take action.

Essential Couple Conversation 7

Fidelity

The last thing you or your stepchild need is another divorce to deal with and all the changes that come with a failed marriage. Where is the fidelity line of no return in your relationship? Meeting an old boyfriend for coffee, intercourse with a stranger, texting, flirting at a party, sharing a laugh with an Ex or asking your beloved for a threesome?

People are flawed and make mistakes. Be very clear on what *exactly* is a deal-breaker for you regarding fidelity. Infidelity is the big killer of many marriages.

> *Define infidelity and cheating clearly and decide if you can be your partner's definition of faithful, not just your definition.*

Do you believe a second chance is available for an otherwise great partner? Would you want a second chance? Try to forgive and forget if you can and rediscover trust in a partner who is sincerely trying to be a better spouse.

Most marriages face some level of infidelity. The ease of connecting on social network sites can cause marital insecurity to increase. Today's slip-up may be yours. A few years from now, your spouse may be challenged. Work through it, don't just throw out the good because someone makes a stupid mistake.

Try to avoid the obvious risky situations and be protective of the family that you are working so hard to build.

In many popular magazines, there are clever articles about how to lie to your partner, how to deceive them and when caught what other lies to tell. Lies that endorse the cruelty of, "Even though we are in this relationship, I'm going to sneak around and say I didn't."

Partners need to hold each other accountable for their half of the relationship. It does not take more strength to resist the desire for someone new by one partner than it does for the other. Women and men struggle with boredom, raging desire or passion equally. The timing is different for men than for women depending on what stage of life, opportunity or emotional health is surfacing.

Women Can Write New Laws

Temptation—the desire for a stranger, a fantasy romance, some excitement, or the neighbor is no less difficult for a woman than a man, yet often in the past, her punishment was worse. American society has tolerated male indiscretion and weakness more easily yet penalized a woman with severe economic and judgmental consequences. Women's looks are said to tempt men to be bad, aggressive or rape, and, therefore, she should be punished for that, too. That sounds ridiculous, yet shades of such chauvinism exist in many religions and archaic government laws around the world. As women rise in political office and as religious leaders, these sometimes-deadly chauvinistic dictums will be rewritten.

Couples are equally accountable for their behavior in this era of deadly sexually transmitted disease. Unprotected sex is a risky weapon. Unprotected intercourse with an infected new lover, even once, could be lethal. If you withhold properly warning your old partner before being sexual with them again, disease could potentially kill them. You must tell the truth and take the consequences of what you have done.

Counseling experience has taught us many powerful and important lessons on the absurdity of life, fully believing the maxim: "You always get caught," and the first law of happiness is: Stop lying.

Couples can recover from infidelity if they sincerely work together. The haunting, obsessing thoughts that continually stab the wronged partner will diminish over time as all memories do and the pain fades. That is when the trust can begin to build again. Don't ask for details. Details pile on more hurt and memories that must be processed and forgotten.

The tender adoration for your "perfect" partner was not sustainable or fair to your partner. As a relationship ages, you and your partner topple from high pedestals of fanciful romantic love to the solid ground of commitment and devotion. Long-lasting true love begins when you accept each other as human, with flaws, weakness, confusion and personal struggles. Keep it real, and romantic once in a while.

If you doubt your ability to be faithful but want to have a good marriage, then you need to seek counseling. Be open about the problem. Your spouse and your stepchild deserve your best effort.

Essential Couple Conversation 8

Discipline

The definition of discipline is teaching. Rewards work far better than punishment. Spanking, hitting, beating your stepchild (or an animal) either breaks their spirit and renders them forever a victim to bullies, or it teaches them how to be violent to less powerful spouses, children, co-workers, or pets. Teaching is not violent, or loud. If your parent did things to you that were cruel and counter-productive, break the chain and be better than your parents with the stepchild in your care.

Carrots not Canes

Your spouse has power, and right now you do not. You will in a few years. Let your spouse handle the discipline until your stepchild cares enough for you to want to please you. Love and respect are what keep your stepchild's behavior in line. Punishment does not work. Reinforcing good behavior, with reward and recognition, work best.

Parental power comes from your stepchild wanting to please you and maintain a good relationship.

At first, parental power is not there for a stepparent. Clear behavior rules posted on the refrigerator help your stepchild understand your family expectations. You do not know what is best for them, or how to make them behave. Your stepchild has not been raised in the same way as you have raised your kids. Your stepchild may have experienced a bioparent's mental or physical trauma, neglect, molestation, drug or alcohol addiction, or the unbearable loss of a parent they loved.

Your job is to support your spouse while he or she parents their children and you parent and discipline yours. Your spouse's methods may be wildly different from yours but be exactly the right discipline for your stepchild in question.

Always select the least harsh, least violent, least physical or least mentally torturous punishment.

Stay Small

Never take away big events from your stepchild like a Disney trip, prom, class trip to Europe, or band camp. Figure out a different punishment and avoid heartbreak that will never be forgotten. Your stepchild will become numb to shouting, severe punishment, name-calling or cursing. When you become wrong in your behavior, your stepchild can justify any of their behavior. You will achieve nothing good, and you need not elevate your stress levels.

If your style is to be a "bully" who pushes people around, you will be intolerant of the quiet listening and positive reinforcement methods of your spouse. Your spouse's discipline methods were functioning before you came along, and your novice opinions may resemble meteors that disturb the status quo. Be a supportive partner to your spouse. When a stepparent gets involved, the added input tends to escalate the conflicts. Unless it directly involves you, let them work things out and have faith your spouse can handle their child.

Never love your biochildren <u>less</u> in an attempt to appear equal.

Never feel guilty for finding it easier to love your biochildren at first, than your new stepchild. Initially, you may not even like your stepchild. It is a bad idea to reveal to your spouse that your stepchild is a terrible thorn in your side. You will break the heart of the one you love.

Until loving feelings catch up to your situation, you can behave "lovingly" toward your stepchild—difficult, but right. Avoid becoming a controlling over-disciplinarian. Ignore ninety-five percent of the conflicts and drama. It is pointless to get dragged into ancient family feuds fraught with rituals of jealousy, greed and rudeness. Guide your stepchild with wisdom and experience, do not hit or spank. Keep quiet about everything that does not directly affect you.

Your stepchild, especially teens, cannot hear you when they are having a meltdown. They are in

fight or flight mode, and their emotions have overwhelmed them.

If a conflict does breakout, your scolding or criticism is futile when deep emotions are unleashed. Say, "We will discuss this later with your parent." Back away and let your stepchild regain a sense of control and safety. In the midst of your stepchild's breakdown, reassure them that, "Everything will be OK eventually. We will find solutions together as a family, and you will be happy again, so calm down." Kids attempt suicide over minor issues, especially nine to twelve-year-old children who cannot envision the future. Reassurance from a calm adult during a crisis can be what saves them. Never escalate a situation with a selfish loss of your temper.

Later, you can discuss the misbehavior calmly without yelling or adding your hysteria to the mix. Let most things slide unless it is going to cause physical harm, breaks established rules or causes irreparable damage. An issue with your stepchild usually disappears in several months as they mature and go on to something new. The more attention you give bad behavior, the more likely it will be repeated. There may be a feeling of skewed power in your stepchild if they can upset a bioparent or stepparent.

Endurance

Remember the long-distance goals, not short-sighted irritations. Your willingness to be vulnerable and let your stepchild see that their words or actions hurt you, or the family, can be helpful, without taking it to a scolding level. Avoid situations where you get mad, and your stepchild becomes defensive and can blame you for over-reacting.

In a little while, they may calm down and see the error of their bad behavior. Sometimes you just sit calmly with relaxed compassion and your peaceful demeanor is transferred to your stepchild. This is far superior teaching than for you to absorb their mood and react on their level of chaos and nonsense drama.

BE the Adult in the Room

If anyone, including the Ex, insists that discipline not be physical, then honor that wish. Sadistic, harsh and cruel treatment of a child has no place in this world no matter what justification a "this is for your own good-sadist parent" tries to argue. A parent's job is to protect their child, nurture and care for them, and teach them to be good kind and fair adults. How does hitting accomplish anything but create another generation of sadistic parenting? If a parent begins to think they must protect their child from you, then you are soon to be out on the curb.

Although your stepchild may push all your buttons, hoping you will lose your cool and turn violent, the choice of your behavior is always your responsibility. No excuses will soothe your spouse if you cross the line of discipline into abuse.

Essential Couple Conversation 9

Religion, Sex & Politics

Polite conversation at social gatherings avoids the topics of religion, sex, and politics. However, these Big Three subjects will cause so much turmoil in a relationship if they are left as unmentionables.

Religion

How important are religious practices to you? Religious practices are <u>not</u> spirituality, believing in a God or Higher Power, or even being a good person. Rather, it is the demonstration of group behavior by attendance at services, kneeling, singing in repetitive unison, making a young vulnerable child an altar boy, dedicating Sundays or Saturdays exclusively to religious activities, wearing costumes of hats, scarves, robes or chains, or strict adherence to words written thousands of years ago. If your spouse is a "flower child" seeking freedom from being told what to do, there will be a struggle between tradition and freedom rooted in deeply held beliefs and disbelief.

If introducing your stepchild to the beauty of gratitude for his or her life through organized religion is crucial to you, then you must express your needs to your spouse now. Otherwise, holidays and weekends will be a battleground for all. If a teen rejects the family religion, rather than shun the teen, listen to their viewpoint and know that with age comes wisdom and different perspectives. The news stories are filled with evangelists, scammers, and pedophiles who prey on the innocence of our hearts seeking to understand life, spirituality and the meaning of our difficult struggles and unbearable losses. People who say they hear God speaking to them are often diagnosed with schizophrenia, yet, many families place holy men's words above their own truth of what they can see is fallacy, facades, lies or deception. Be aware that your spouse's beliefs may conflict with what you were taught. Avoid insisting that your stepchild participate in your customs and religious practices.

Sex

So great in the beginning but then comes the fading … as the relationship settles into a marriage with children, sex cannot stay your top priority. Romance is usurped by errands, homework, birthdays, dishes, shopping, meals, bills, pets, school events, and health issues. Everyone else's needs encroach on what was just the two of you and your passionate desire for each other.

No relationship can maintain the fever-pitch of passion. This does not mean your relationship is in trouble, but rather that your relationship is maturing and changing.

People addicted to the thrill of passion must keep looking for new partners to substitute for the old to maintain the rush. As love settles into a long-term relationship, the passionate moments may become less frequent because of busy lives—not the loss of love or desire. The value you feel for your relationship must be for the whole relationship, not just the hot sex part.

Demanding more sex from a fatigued partner is the surest way to get less sex and a partner who withdraws even more. A natural balance keeps love tender and increases the chance that passion will flame. If you need more sex, masturbate; if you need more intimacy, communicate.

Be grateful for any lovemaking you do have and enjoy each other without pressure to perform or satisfy your imaginary "must have" sex. Sex is a want, not a need, no matter how intense.

Politics

Did you pick a team and no matter how many crooks or bad decisions your team makes, you refuse to change? Try to pick the candidate, not just a straight party ticket. Enjoy each other's differing opinions on where our leaders should take the future of our country. Alternate the input you listen to, read newspapers, change channels, take a college course and study political history. Talk to young people and old people, different races, and religions from your own and open your mind to leaders with new ideas.

Essential Couple Conversation 10

What Do I Want?

You may feel alone and isolated as your spouse is showered with love, attention, and hugs from your stepchild. Your stepchild may greet you with, "Where's my Mom?" or "Where's my Dad?" questions that make you feel insignificant. That is not about you, that is about your stepchild's insecurity needs that are easily met by connecting with their parent. You fell in love with your spouse and dreamed of your romantic relationship. Your spouse may want to meet your needs, but he or she is spread thin by needy children. You may only get crumbs of the feast you envisioned but do *value the crumbs*.

Do you believe that love is limited, and your stepchild takes away some of what belongs to you? Then you may experience jealousy when your spouse shows love and affection for your stepchild. That is possession, not love.

Love is more like a river without end or breadth or depth. There is enough love to go around.

Enjoy the love that abounds in your world—even if it is not directly aimed at you.

Control is a constant factor in all relationships. Kids can wear you down with their attempts to control the family. See this as a normal part of growing up and remind them they are not your parent or your boss.

Some single parents are so desperate for help that they marry to acquire a co-parent more than a lover. Even if that is not true, the unlimited demands of children can make a stepparent feel like they are a babysitter instead of a partner. Plan dates without your stepchild even if you go to a park with a cup of coffee and hold hands. Nourish your love when you can but go into stepparenting with your eyes wide open ... you are second, not first. In a lonely, crazy world, second is still wonderful. Believe that every day the household is getting better. Some days that will seem impossible and somedays the new family system will work.

Do you feel like your life is passing you by? What are you running after—money, power, adoration, fame? Maybe you are missing moments of richness, love and simple joy as you run hard towards unattainable goals.

The main reason you are unhappy is not what is going on around you, but it is the meaningless, often urgent, negative thoughts that flood your mind.

Negativity binds and blinds us from serenity and the peace of contented simple mindfulness. Stop and "smell the roses" of life whenever you can.

Are you absorbing other people's urgent needs and desires and discounting what is important to your happiness? Will your needs, opinions, and observations be welcomed and valued or ignored? Is your view of your current life situation one filled with gratitude? Do you say to yourself, "I am so lucky to be in this relationship, to have a stepchild to nurture and someday love, or do you get out of bed, sigh, swear and start your day?

Be grateful to your parents for your life and your ability to think, move and reason. The decisions and sacrifices they made in their lives made it possible for you to know life. Perhaps that is all your parents could give you. So, forgive the past—all of it. As an adult, it is time to lose the grudges and bitterness for people who failed you in the past. A large majority of the people in your future may also disappoint you, betray you or hurt you, too. That comes with life. If you keep your mind on the failures of the past, then your world becomes about failure. Shine a dazzling smile into your life and let the negativity go. We can't see around the corner. We have no true vision of our future. We often only envision future events based on the past. But there are infinite solutions to every challenge and a surprising and wonderful future may be just around that corner if you set your mind free to change, to be new.

Find something, anything, to appreciate about your life, your spouse, your stepchild, or your hectic home life, and you will transform your negative attitude—and theirs.

Even if your efforts are not met in kind by other family members, you can reduce your struggle, your frustration and feel happier. If a problem seems insurmountable and you are at your wit's end, there is a path through all obstacles with a good counselor or trusted elder.

It takes so much courage to be willing to get your feelings hurt, to be disappointed, uncomfortable or fail again and again. If you are strong in your purpose, know the "why" of your choices, you can keep your stepparenting perspective. Your job is to help raise your stepchild in as large, or as limited a role as best benefits the family. Your stepchild is under no obligation to you, other than to be polite and fair within their family dynamics, and to make a little room in their lives for their parent's new spouse. Hopefully, they will make room in their hearts for someone new, who cares for them and wants the best in life for them.

An excellent way to approach life is to start believing that you are lucky, that your life is bountiful. Be thankful for the opportunities and for the people who are coming into your life to love you. Maybe they are already here.

You may find there is a short route to happiness when you choose to feel grateful. Your stepchild will adopt your attitude, either good or bad. Be a leader by filling your heart with gratitude. See what looking forward with hope, and an attitude of gratitude can do to change your world and the heart of your stepchild.

*Congratulations.
You did it!
You are a
wonderful
stepparent.*

Show your love and gratitude to your spouse, your biochildren, and your stepchild and watch your family thrive.

–DR. MOLLY BARROW

25 ESSENTIAL STEPPARENTING RULES TO BLEND YOUR NEW MARRIAGE AND PROTECT YOUR SANITY

Rule 1 .... p.13
Avoid sitting directly across from your stepchild during meals.

Rule 2 .... p.17
Take your own car whenever possible.

Rule 3 .... p. 21
Never compete with the Ex for your stepchild's love.

Rule 4 .... p. 25
Try to avoid moving into your stepchild's house.

Rule 5 .... p. 29
Avoid entering your stepchild's bedroom.

Rule 6 .... p. 33
Never interfere with the natural grief over their broken original family.

Rule 7 . . . . *p. 37*
A budget can help contain the guilt reaction of your spouse.

Rule 8 . . . . *p. 41*
Never talk badly about the Ex.

Rule 9 . . . . *p. 45*
Be certain that you give your time, money, and effort as a gift.

Rule 10 . . . . *p. 49*
Make time for romance with your spouse.

Rule 11 . . . . *p. 53*
Avoid sharing a bathroom with your stepchild.

Rule 12 . . . . *p. 57*
Do not discipline your stepchild for the first few years.

Rule 13 . . . . *p. 61*
Try hard to be friends with the Ex.

Rule 14 . . . . *p. 65*
Avoid sexual discussions, interactions, jokes or excessive flattery.

Rule 15 . . . . *p. 69*
Protect yourself from your stepchild's noise whenever possible.

Rule 16 . . . . *p. 73*
Never let your stepchild win your allegiance away from your spouse.

Rule 17 .... p. 77
Never schedule dates with your spouse during your stepchild's events.

Rule 18 .... p. 81
Never allow the competition to work the kid angle.

Rule 19 .... p. 85
Never get involved in original family arguments.

Rule 20 .... p. 89
Beware of some children's movies.

Rule 21 .... p. 93
Include grandparents as often as possible.

Rule 22 .... p. 97
Never give up your basic human rights to gain points.

Rule 23 .... p. 101
Never make your stepchild the brunt of your jokes, shame or put downs.

Rule 24 .... p. 105
Learn to love your stepchild's pet, too.

Rule 25 .... p. 109
Believe every day you will blend.

10 ESSENTIAL COUPLE CONVERSATIONS TO END CONFLICT

Conversation 1 ....p. 133
Family Expectations

Conversation 2 ....p. 135
Communication Strengths

Conversation 3 ....p. 139
Family Finances

Conversation 4 ....p. 136
The Ex

Conversation 5 ....p. 149
Time Allocation

Conversation 6 ....p. 155
What's Best for Your Stepchild?

Conversation 7 ....p. 163
Fidelity

Conversation 8 ....p. 167
Discipline

Conversation 9 ....p. 173
Religion, Sex & Politics

Conversation 10.....................p. 177
What Do I Want?

Molly Barrow Ph.D.

TAKE THE TEST

The Matchlines Relationship Test

$25.00

GO to: www.matchlinestest.com

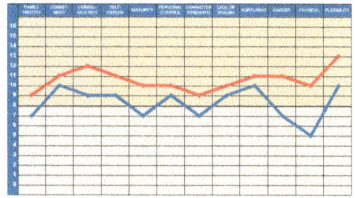

ABOUT THE AUTHOR

Dr. Molly Barrow holds a Ph.D. in clinical psychology and is an authority on relationship and psychological topics. Dr. Barrow is the founder and executive director of the IMAGINE Children's Health Center, a critical care 501(c)(3) non-profit dedicated to children's health (www.imaginechc.com). She is a member of the American Psychological Association and is a licensed mental health counselor in private practice treating children, families, and adults.

Dr. Barrow has appeared as an expert in film and documentaries, and on KTLA Impact, NBC news, Web M.D., PBS In Focus, WBZT talk radio, and hosted the *Dr. Molly Barrow Show* on PRN for three years. She has been quoted in *O Magazine, Psychology Today, Newsday, Oprah.com, Tesh.com, Parenting Blog, People.com, AIA.org, Newlyweds.com, The Nest, MSN.com, Yahoo.com, Match.com, N Magazine, Women's Health*, and *Women's World*. Relationship analysis and healthy relationship advice for couples, families, and business are available at: http://www.mollybarrowphd.com. Dr. Barrow is a mother, a stepmother, and a stepchild.

Molly Barrow Ph.D.

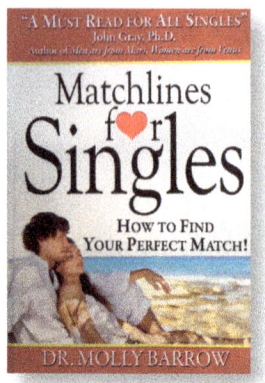

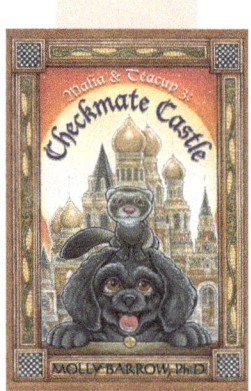

Books by Molly Barrow, Ph.D.

Relationship Books for Adults:
Matchlines for Singles
Matchlines: A Revolutionary New Way of Looking at Relationships and Making the Right Choices in Love
StepParenting Essentials: A Guide to Love, Blend and Survive
mollybarrowphd.com

Children's Self-esteem Building Adventure Series:
Malia and Teacup: Awesome African Adventure
Malia and Teacup: Kingdom of the Thunder Dragon
Malia and Teacup: Checkmate Castle
Malia and Teacup Out on a Limb (Early Reader)
maliaandteacupbooks.com

To Order Books:
amazon.com, barnesandnoble.com
barringerpublishing.com

Professional Relationship Tests:
Relationship Compatibility Matchlines Test for Couples
Who is the Right One for Me? Matchlines Test for Singles
matchlinestest.com

A portion of all book sales will be donated to the

A 501(c)3 Charity

Dedicated to the mental health of children.

EIN 47-1594923

www.ingramcontent.com/pod-product-compliance
Lightning Source LLC
Chambersburg PA
CBHW042132160426
43199CB00021B/2882